# ABRAHAM LINCOLN

# MAKERS OF HISTORY

Published in 1965

CHATHAM
*J. H. Plumb*

SIR CHRISTOPHER WREN
*John Summerson*

ABRAHAM LINCOLN
*Herbert Agar*

*Abraham Lincoln in 1858*
*By permission of Frederick Meserve*

MAKERS OF HISTORY

# ABRAHAM LINCOLN

*by*

HERBERT AGAR

*Archon Books*

HAMDEN, CONNECTICUT

1965

*First published in 1952*
*First published in the 'Makers of History' Series 1965*

FOR BARBIE

*Library of Congress Catalog Card number*
*65-19158*

# Contents

# Plates

# Maps

# Introduction

Lincoln is a secular saint for millions of people, world-wide, who believe in human dignity; but he has often been canonized for the wrong reasons. He was not, in fact, the Great Emancipator. He freed very few slaves, and he would have been content to free none at all if that had been the price of saving the American Union. He deplored slavery, of course; and he knew that if he saved the Union the slaves would one day be free. But he put first things first. The Federal Union, if it survived, must soon set itself to abolish servitude. The Southern Confederacy, if it won the war for secession, would maintain its outmoded system of bondage until the last grievous hour. So Lincoln—the Union-preserver—became hated by abolitionist and slave-holder alike: too soft and accommodating for the first, too stern and unyielding for the latter.

With his uncanny sense of politics, he could easily have enjoyed a quick, cheap triumph over these enemies—a settlement which settled nothing. He chose to play for the far stakes, the long-term stakes. Thus he saved the Union, geographically. He might have saved it spiritually as well—not posthumously, but in his own life-time—had he been allowed to live. He alone might have persuaded a Congress maddened by victory to forget revenge and to copy Grant's chivalry toward Lee's surrendered army at Appomattox.

Why then is Lincoln who was reviled when alive, and who died with his work half-done, a hero for most men who aspire to freedom? He was as devious as many politicians when it came to imposing his will—although his will, extraordinarily, seemed often to be selfless. He seized power as boldly and

7

used it as firmly as many dictators—although he sometimes confessed what he had done, and why, and asked to be exculpated in retrospect. The South pictured him as an implacable tyrant out of the Roman civil wars, rather than as a saviour of Democracy. Why is this picture false? Why do we now revere Lincoln to such a point that we can scarcely be bothered arguing about his shortcomings?

First, he was humble, with a humility which all sensitive men admire but which few attain. Second, he was gentle. If possible, he would protect his most injurious enemies from the knowledge of their own folly. He knew too much, and felt too deeply, ever to be needlessly cruel. He could not hate his opponent wholeheartedly, or applaud himself. And third, he was lonely with the deep loneliness of those who see too far. Most men hide in the midst of crowds, weakly gregarious, frightened that they can neither understand their neighbour nor hope to be understood. But Lincoln was unafraid, and thus reassuring. He accepted the painful facts of human depravity without recrimination. For example, he knew that his Cabinet—which he chose for merit when possible, for politics when necessary—thought him gawky, ill-mannered, inexperienced, unworthy of the majestic occasion. He paid no heed—not because he felt superior, but because he lived night-long with so many genuine troubles that he had little time to fret about a few ambition-ridden men.

"Did Stanton" (the Secretary of War) "tell you I was a damn fool?" said Lincoln to an astonished tale-bearer: "Then I expect I must be one, for he is almost always right and generally says what he means."

In *John Brown's Body*, Stephen Vincent Benet gives Lincoln a mild complaint against the men who pestered him all day long and who knew exactly what he ought to do:

> *They come to me and talk about God's will*
> *In righteous deputations and platoons,*
> *Day after day, laymen and ministers . . .*

8

# INTRODUCTION

*God's will is General This and Senator That,*
*God's will is those poor coloured fellows' will . . .*
*But all of them are sure they know God's will.*
*I am the only man who does not know it.*

Most of all, perhaps, we revere Lincoln because his tragic sense of life was wedded to a love of jest, of wild folly—a love which alarmed the sober men who surrounded him. He is our folk-hero, not only because he faced the worst or because he suffered for the sins of others, but also because he still enjoyed the crazy nonsense of human incongruity. His thoughtful, sombre face—which his wife called "his Photographer's face"—is proof that he carried the burden of his office and of his time. But we have never seen his other face, which his friends loved—his face of fun. "When he has made his remark," wrote Ralph Waldo Emerson, "he looks at you with great satisfaction, and shows all his white teeth, and laughs." Lincoln was not the broken-hearted clown of melodrama, who laughs in order not to despair. Lincoln saw life steadily; he mourned its indurate cruelty; he laughed because life is often funny.

One day a clutter of politicians came to him, insisting that he appoint a friend of theirs as Commissioner to the Sandwich Islands. The man was unwell, they said; but the climate of those fortunate isles would restore him. Lincoln answered: "I am sorry to say that there are eight applicants for that place, and they are all sicker than your man." Another day one of his endless advisers—who knew precisely what God thought, and whom the Holy Ghost approved—asked him if he enjoyed being President. "Well," said Lincoln, "you know about the man who was tarred and feathered and ridden out of town on a rail? Someone asked him how he liked it, and he said that if wasn't for the honour of the thing he would much rather walk."

By saving the Union, Lincoln renewed the work of George

Washington, the Father of his country. By aggrandizing the powers of the Presidency—to win a war which could so easily and so often have been lost—Lincoln set the pattern for the future of American politics. Thenceforward, whenever the Republic was in mortal danger—whether from foreign foes or from collapse at home—the President, if popular and bold, could take charge. Thenceforth the division of powers, painstakingly imposed upon the written Constitution, could be overridden in a dark hour—so long as the people who were aware of the darkness asked for light. Woodrow Wilson understood this, and Franklin Roosevelt, and Mr. Truman.

Because of Lincoln's daring, Lincoln's re-invigoration of his office, the United States may well survive until a big trouble coincides with a small President, or until the American people choose laziness and conformity instead of the nerve-racking argument, discord and committee-work which are the meaning of Democracy.

## II

In the spring of 1860 the two great regions of the United States drifted toward civil war in a mood which reminds us of our world in 1965. A mere list of the failures to understand the "other side" gives a solemn warning of how life repeats itself.

1. On the issue of slavery each side "knew" that it alone was right. The South "knew" that the slaves were better cared-for, in soul and body, than any other Negroes on earth. The North "knew" that slavery was sin and that men who defended it were hypocrites or knaves. The South "knew" that factory hands in Pennsylvania were treated like sub-slaves. The North "knew" that in Alabama slaves were treated like cattle.

2. Although the expansion or containment of slavery was the immediate and concrete problem, most politicians chose to argue about abstractions: federalism, or majority rule, or the "sovereignty" of a State. The words had different mean-

ings in Massachusetts and in Virginia; yet each State "knew" that its own meaning was correct, and that the other side was diabolically distorting the truth.

3. Since each side was grossly self-righteous, passions and prejudice mounted incontinently. The unhealthy hatreds bred fear of treachery. And the fear bred mass hysteria. We cannot understand the United States in 1860 if we ignore this hysteria. Southerners (who still controlled the government at Washington) talked as if they had already been invaded and as if their sufferings were those of the Dutch under the Duke of Alba. Northerners talked as if the cultivated citizens of Virginia and South Carolina were the worst men alive, with whom it was an insult to be linked. Even the far-seeing Emerson called the South a "barbarous community."

4. The fear of treachery led each side to mistake defensive measures for aggression. The South "knew" that the North meant to abolish slavery by force. The North "knew" that the South meant to impose it in the territories and upon conquered islands in the Caribbean. The fact that in both camps a small group of extremists did hold such views made the fear more deadly. The fact that the majority everywhere longed for peace and compromise and union was well-nigh forgotten. Each region saw the other as a potential thief, itself as an innocent victim beset by scoundrels.

Such was the mood of the nation when Abraham Lincoln was first nominated for the presidency: Lincoln, the least prejudiced, or hysterical, or self-righteous of men.

Failure of leadership had been the American tragedy during the 1850's. Moderation, mollification, the humility to admit mistakes and the generosity to make concessions: these qualities had been missing both in the North and in the South. But they were pre-eminently the qualities of Lincoln. They helped him to win the war which he was too late to prevent. Had he not been murdered in 1865 they would have helped him to make the peace for which he pleaded—"with malice toward none, with charity for all."

### III

Carlyle tells us that the mark of a Hero is that "the great Fact of Existence is great to him. Fly as he will he cannot get out of the awful presence of this Reality. His mind is so made: he is great by that, first of all. Fearful and wonderful, real as life, real as death, is this Universe to him. Though all men should forget its truth, and walk in a vain show, he cannot. At all moments the Flame-image glares in upon him; undeniable, there, there!"

The words might have been written about Lincoln, who could never escape (except when telling funny stories) from the obsessive questions: "What can we know, what ought we to do, what may we hope?" He brooded over Carlyle's "great Fact of Existence" from his twelfth year onward—therefore he was always learning, always growing in wisdom and moral strength. He loved truth no matter how painful, and sought it faithfully.

A lawyer described him once in court, "sitting alone in a corner of the bar, remote from anyone, wrapped in abstraction and gloom. He seemed to be pursuing in his mind some specific painful subject, regularly and systematically through various sinuosities, and his sad face would assume, at times, deeper phases of grief. No relief came till he was roused by the adjournment of court, when he emerged from his cage of gloom, like one awakened from sleep."

Carlyle was right: the Hero "cannot get out of the awful presence of Reality . . . Though all men should forget its truth, and walk in a vain show, he cannot." We have only to look at the photographs of Lincoln to see that the statement fits. When his twelve-year-old son, Tad, stood beside the coffin at the White House, he was told that Lincoln had gone to heaven. Tad is reported to have answered: "Then I am glad, for he was not really happy here."

# * 1 *
## The Formative Years
### *1809-1849*

---

ABRAHAM LINCOLN was born in Kentucky in 1809, not far from where Jefferson Davis, his war-time enemy and his eternal opposite, had been born the previous year. The two men were to become rival Presidents and rival Commanders-in-Chief within the once-United States. Both were born to frontier poverty. But the Davis family moved south to Mississippi and prospered, while the Lincolns moved north to Indiana and remained almost destitute.

Within a few years Davis had become a well-to-do planter, an " aristocrat," the spokesman for a proud oligarchy, while Lincoln in his early thirties wrote to his best friend: " I am so poor and make so little headway in the world that I drop back in a month of idleness as much as I gain in a year's saving." Yet the slow-maturing Lincoln saved the Union, giving new hope to free men everywhere; and the brilliant Davis frittered away the Confederacy. The contrast reminds us of Arnold Toynbee's thesis that a harsh environment, if it does not kill, calls forth a strength which easy circumstances smother.

The rich cotton lands of Mississippi—exploited by slave labour—offered quick wealth to the lucky. And the climate was an invitation to leisure:

> *The white wolf-winter, hungry and frore,*
> *Can prowl the North by a frozen door,*
> *But here we have fed him on bacon fat,*
> *And he sleeps by the stove like a lazy cat.*

There was not much sleeping by the stove in Lincoln's childhood. His grandfather had emigrated from Virginia to Kentucky, where he was killed by the Indians while opening a farm in the primeval forest: the " dark and bloody ground " of pioneer legend. Thomas Lincoln, the father of Abraham, was trained as a carpenter but farming was his true vocation. He was forever deserting one run-down homestead for another. He married Nancy Hanks, who may have been an illegitimate child. Her father is in any case unknown—and those who believe that genius must be in part a product of heredity have a free field for guessing whence came the grandeur of Nancy's son, Abraham.

When Lincoln was seven the family left Kentucky to try its luck across the Ohio River in Indiana. The first winter was spent in a lean-to, enclosed on three sides but open on the South to the fierce Middle Western weather. Indiana (and the neighbouring Illinois, where the Lincolns were soon to move) has a " continental " climate with great heat and afflicting cold. " I am sure this land was settled before the Lord was willing," said one pioneer woman. And Will Herndon, who was to become Lincoln's law-partner, recalled the hardships of his frontier youth with loathing. " Words cannot tell this life," he said. " The prairies of Illinois are watered with the tears, and enriched by the graves, of her women. The first generation lived on mush and pork . . . Just as our corn was ripe, the bears would strip the ears; just as the pumpkins grew golden, herds of deer would hollow out the gourds."

In Iowa, across the Mississippi River from Illinois, on a beautiful evening of early winter, the author of this book heard a garage owner begging a young couple not to set out westward, that night, in their well-heated automobile. They had a lonely road before them, he said, and the air " smelled dangerous." Also there had been blizzard warnings on the radio. But the couple persisted, never having known the cruel prairies. Six hours later the woman was dead and the man had lost both his hands through freezing.

Though Indiana is not quite so sudden and extreme, it is no country for a " half-faced camp " in winter—or for the floorless, doorless, windowless log-cabin with which the camp was replaced. Nancy Hanks Lincoln survived for two years, dying in 1818 when her son was nine.

The next year Thomas Lincoln married again, and Abe found that the fairy-tales were all wrong: the stepmother, instead of being wicked, became his chief strength and support. She was Sarah Johnston of Kentucky, a widow with three children. She brought some furniture and some ambition to the backwoods cabin. She even insisted on the luxury of a floor and a few windows. She believed in education and fostered

Lincoln's thirst for knowledge—a thirst which his father is said to have regarded as a dishonourable fever, to be rigorously suppressed.

" I suppose Abe is still fooling hisself with eddication," said Thomas Lincoln many years later. " I tried to stop it, but he had got that fool idea in his head, and it can't be got out."[1]  Yet all the schooling Abe acquired in his life did not add up to one full year.  In order to " fool himself with education " he had to borrow books in a community where they were as scarce as dinosaur-eggs, and to study them in a tiny hut which was often inhabited by nine people: the father, the stepmother with her three children, Abe's sister Sarah, a couple of cousins' and himself.

Luckily, although Lincoln's books were few they were exactly right for a boy who had to teach himself: the Bible, *Robinson Crusoe*, *The Pilgrim's Progress*, *Æsop's Fables*, Pike's *Arithmetic*, Grimshaw's *History of the United States*, Scott's *Lessons in Elocution*, the *Revised Laws of Indiana*, Weem's *Life of Washington*, and later (by a seeming miracle which may have done much to determine his career) a complete set of the volumes which in those days were almost sacred writ to the young Americans who wished to study law: Blackstone's *Commentaries on the Laws of England*.

Blackstone he found in an old barrel which he had bought for fifty cents from a man who was migrating to the West and who had no room for it in his wagon.  The man said the barrel held nothing of value, and Lincoln

---

[1] This was reported by Lincoln's cousin, Dennis Hanks.  Other contemporaries, however, have testified that Tom Lincoln took pride in his son's ability to read.

Plate 1. Lincoln's first school. The cabin had no windows, and the children had no books: they had to repeat what the teacher said

Plate 2. The Lincoln home in Indiana. At times nine people were living together in this one-roomed cabin

*Plate 3.   Ulysses S. Grant*
from Stefan Lorant's
'Lincoln, A Picture Story of His Life'

did not even empty it until months later. Then, he tells us, " I began to read these famous works . . . Never in my whole life was my mind so thoroughly absorbed. I read until I had devoured them."

By the time of this treasure-trove the Lincoln family had moved from Indiana to Illinois. Abe had come of age, had made two flatboat trips down the Ohio and Mississippi rivers to New Orleans, had parted from his father, and had set up for himself in the tiny village of New Salem, about twenty miles north-west of Springfield, Illinois. At New Salem (which in 1831 was about the size of Chicago, with a few hundred inhabitants) Lincoln earned a scant living by splitting rails, working in a " general store," acting as postmaster and as deputy surveyor.

At New Salem he is said to have fallen in love with Ann Rutledge, who was engaged to another man and who insisted on waiting to see whether her fiancé had deserted her or had merely forgotten to write. While waiting, Ann caught an unidentified fever (which was probably typhoid) and died. There have been many legends about the effects upon Lincoln of this romance; but our scanty first-hand information would give no ground for taking the story very seriously.

## II

During his six years at New Salem Abe Lincoln's character took form. He grew into a solemn, awkward young man who had no time for liquor and little for girls but who loved the male companionship of the country store or the court-house—the clubs of that lonely frontier world. When he was not reading, or brooding over what he had seen and read, or earning his precarious living, he was talking politics with his men friends—or talking philosophy which they did not recognise as philosophy because it was enriched by tales from the Bible or from local legend, or by bawdy stories which were repeated not because they were bawdy but because they were pointful and hilarious.

With his love of solitude and his shyness, his love for poetry and his deep reserve, he combined a piety towards the animal kingdom and an other-worldliness in regard to property which would make him sound priggish if we did not know that men everywhere sought him out for the fun of his company. After his first successful shot at a wild turkey he could never bring himself to hunt game. Neither could he bring himself to take wealth seriously. " He had no money sense," said Will Herndon; " He never developed even a reasonable desire to be rich. Wealth remained, in his view ' a superfluity of the things one does not want.' " A friend once chided him, " You might have made money entering land at a dollar and a half an acre." " Yes," said Lincoln, " that is true —but I never had any money sense." This was not the customary point of view on that land-hungry, land-speculating frontier. Yet Lincoln, the most complex of men, was not wholly unconcerned with material things. He became a man of modest but substantial property, an able and ambitious lawyer, as well as an able and ambitious politician.

Lincoln was a hero to the roughest frontier rowdies,

such as the " Clary Grove Boys " at New Salem. When he went to the Black Hawk war against an Indian tribe (in which he claimed to have seen no blood that was not drawn by mosquitoes) he was unanimously elected captain of his company. And when he first stood for the State legislature (unsuccessfully) he received two hundred and seventy-seven votes out of the three hundred and four which were cast by his neighbours.

Lincoln won faith and affection because his social awkwardness was combined with an irresistible humour: " the balance-pole of his genius that enabled him to cross the most giddy heights without losing his head." His mouth at one moment might suggest a mask of baffled pain and at the next an impudent broad pleasure in the folly of life. He became a famous story-teller throughout the State of Illinois. He could keep the men round the stove in a village store in ribald laughter indefinitely. He could make nonsense of a serious argument with a moment's mimicry. And although he was known for his thoughtful kindness to witnesses in court, if his anger was roused he could make a witness look so silly that the jury would pay no further heed.

The sudden crazy humour was irresistible—the homely anecdote side by side with the laborious honesty, the slow search for exact truth which Lincoln brought to every subject. As Carl Sandburg says, " he talked to thousands of people as if he and another man were driving in a buggy across the prairie, exchanging their thoughts."

And Lincoln had another asset in that rough community: he had grown into a giant of strength, six feet four in height, powerful as the great trees which he had spent so much of his youth in felling and splitting, a champion wrestler who could take pity on a wild beast and no man would dare laugh. With his grey eyes in their deep-set cavities, his coarse black hair forever rumpled, his long neck and gangling limbs, big ears and heavily seamed skin, he was a striking figure—ugly or attractive depending on the fire within him and the sympathy of the beholder.

Herndon said that Lincoln " looked woe-struck," and that " the whole man, body and mind, worked against more or less friction, and creaked as if it wanted oiling." Yet others, seeing him transfigured in the midst of a speech, called him beautiful. Francis Grierson, who heard one of Lincoln's debates in 1856 with Senator Douglas, described him as follows:

" And now Abraham Lincoln, the man who, in 1830, undertook to split for Mrs. Nancy Miller four hundred rails for every yard of brown jean died with walnut bark that would be required to make him a pair of trousers, the flatboatman, local stump-speaker and country lawyer, rose from his seat, stretched his long bony limbs upwards as if to get them into working order, and stood like some solitary pine on a lonely summit, very tall, very dark, very gaunt, and very rugged, his swarthy features stamped with a sad serenity, and the instant he began to speak the ungainly mouth lost its heaviness, the half-listless eyes attained a wondrous power, and the people stood bewildered and breathless under the natural magic. . . . There were moments when he seemed all legs and feet, and again he appeared all head and neck; yet every look of the deep-set eyes, every movement of the prominent jaw, every wave of the hard-gripping hand, produced an impression, and before he had spoken twenty minutes the conviction took possession of thousands that here was the prophetic man of the present and the political saviour of the future. . . . A man so ungainly, so natural, so earnest, and so forcible, had no place in his mental economy for the thing called vanity." [1]

Did Lincoln communicate an unearthly charm or an ugly and earthly strength? Perhaps his friend Speed gave the best answer: " Mr. Lincoln was so unlike all the men I had ever known before or seen or known since that there is no one to whom I can compare him." Beginning with his New Salem days, when his neighbours voted for him almost unanimously, the news had been slowly spreading from the remoteness of central Illinois that a man had been born into America who saw life steadily, prophetically, and who seemed to be without evil in his heart.

We do not know how such news spreads. In spite of the polls and the advertising men, public opinion fortunately remains a mystery. Long before Lincoln could aspire to challenge the great Senator Douglas, a little frontier preacher chose as his text: " For they shall cry unto the Lord because of the oppressors. And He shall send them a saviour, and a great one, and He shall deliver them." And at the end of his sermon, to a half-scandalised and half pro-slavery audience, the preacher said: " En *who* shall deliver them? Do any of ye know?

[1] *The Valley of Shadows* (1948 edition), pp. 197-8.

Brethering, thar ain't but one human creatur' equal to it, en thet air Abraham Lincoln. The Lord hez called him!"

To-day, as we review the famous and implausible tale of Lincoln's progress from the backwoods to the White House, the preacher seems right. Either the Lord had called him or the democratic system had suddenly chosen the best man—the one man who could save it. In view of the carefully planned mediocrity of the three Presidents who preceded Lincoln, the supernatural explanation is the more credible.

## III

When Lincoln first asked for the votes of his fellow-citizens he made a characteristic speech: " I have been solicited by many friends to become a candidate for the Legislature. My politics are short and sweet, like the old woman's dance. I am in favor of a national bank. I am in favor of the internal-improvements system and a high protective tariff. These are my sentiments and political principles. If elected, I shall be thankful, if not, it will be all the same." [1]

He was twenty-three years old, and in a few words he had said all that was needed. He had identified himself as a follower of Henry Clay and as a Whig. The year was 1832 and Andrew Jackson (the hero of the Democratic Party) was finishing his first term as President. Jackson was the best-loved and best-hated man in American public life.

[1] This version of the speech was written from memory by A. Y. Ellis in 1865.

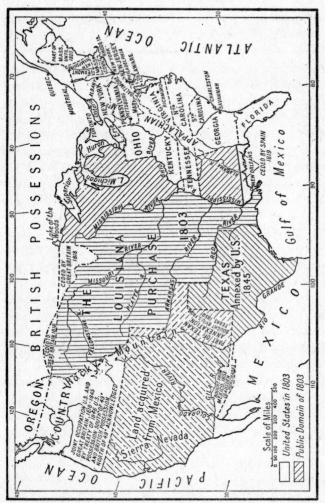

*Territorial Expansion of the United States, 1803–1853*

He was especially hated by Henry Clay, who had just returned to the Senate after two years in retirement to lead the opposition and (he vainly hoped) to capture the presidency. A brilliant and dashing Kentuckian, Clay had been a national leader ever since 1810. Among his many famous deeds which made Lincoln his supporter was the Missouri Compromise of 1820, which was thought to have " solved " the problem of slavery—or at least to have taken it out of politics. The Compromise —which Clay had manœuvred through the House of Representatives—declared that no new slave States should be created in the public domain north of latitude 36° 30'; that is, north of the southern boundary of Missouri. If it had endured, there would have been no Civil War. But it was broken—inevitably broken— because of America's dynamic thrust towards the West.

The waning institution of slavery would have caused no political strife if the United States had kept her original boundaries. The Union of 1789 consisted of thirteen States (or ex-colonies) plus a huge tract of land between the western boundaries of these States and the Mississippi River. Some of the States had nebulous claims to some of this land; but by 1802 it had all been ceded to the Federal Government. This " public domain " was divided by Congress into " territories." The territories were smoothly absorbed into the Union, with the full privileges of States, as soon as they had enough inhabitants.

The northern territories—settled chiefly from New England and New York—became free States. The territories south of the Ohio River—settled chiefly from

Virginia, Georgia, and the two Carolinas—became slave States. There was no serious friction, although the North was dominated by industry and freehold farming, the South by slave-based plantations. By 1819 both regions had expanded to the Mississippi River and each region comprised twelve States. Most men believed that the demon of regional jealousy had been exorcised.

But in 1803 President Jefferson had bought from Napoleon the western empire which was called Louisiana, and which is now divided into thirteen States. This doubled the size of the Union and increased the public domain four-fold.[1] There, in the new West, sectional bitterness became inflamed. Which region, which system of labour, was to exploit this virgin land?

When a western territory was ready to become a State, should it be a slave State if it chose? Or must slavery be confined within the old borders, where it would die in no long time because of the ruinous effect of slave-labour upon the soil? If the majority decided upon confinement, would the Southern minority accept exclusion from the common lands? Or would the South seek to break the Union which thus deprived her?

Jefferson, when he made the Louisiana Purchase, did not foresee these questions—which were raised relentlessly and repeatedly by the nation's march to the Pacific and which dominated Lincoln's political life— because Jefferson strangely believed the United States would need a thousand years to expand as far as the Mississippi. Yet seventeen years after his fateful Purchase

[1] This new public domain was the land to which Clay's Missouri Compromise applied.

the first trans-Mississippi State was demanding entrance to the Union—with a Constitution which permitted slavery.[1]

On what terms, with what boundaries, were the North and the South (free farmers and slave plantations) to face each other across the great river? This was the question that Clay's Compromise sought to answer—by admitting Missouri with slavery, but adding that her *southern* boundary, continued westwards, was to be the dividing line between the two systems for all future States.

But this, too, ignored or underestimated the speed and passion of America's drive towards the West. Backed by the new power of the industrial revolution, the greatest mass migration in history was under way and it would stop for no man's convenience. Twenty-five years after Missouri the vast domain of Texas joined the Union as a State. The next year the Oregon treaty with Great Britain brought the United States to the Pacific. And two years later the Mexican War established her present boundaries.[2] Another public domain, as large as the Louisiana Purchase had now been added—another source of sectional envy and contention. No human foresight, no man-made institutions, could cope with such an explosion of energy, such an imperial march.

Lincoln himself belonged to the first " West." His pioneering took place east of the Mississippi. When he was born there were no American settlers beyond the river—only a few explorers and some nomadic hunters

[1] Louisiana, admitted as a slave State in 1812, is partly east and partly west of the river.

[2] Except for a strip of land in what is now Arizona and New Mexico, which was bought in 1853.

and trappers. Yet by the time he was thirty-seven the American flag was planted on the shores of the Pacific 2,000 miles west of New Salem. And by the time he was forty-one, California was a full-fledged State within the Union.

## IV

As we shall see, Clay's Compromise of 1820 was the first of a series of such efforts—all promoted by the much-admired Kentuckian—to preserve and strengthen the federal Union by political concessions, political adroitness, by postponing the major issues between the sections in the hope that with increasing prosperity the issues would settle themselves. Clay devoted his life to Union-saving, and for this Lincoln loved him. Lincoln, too, sought always to diminish tension, to make a moral climate in which the problems of regional or class interest could be discussed in friendliness. And for both men the Union was the chief purpose of politics. If the Union endured, economic and social clashes could be resolved. If the Union perished, the American experiment must perish. So Lincoln, who had been brought up a Democrat, and who now lived in a state which was Democratic, entered politics defiantly as a Whig.

Since slavery was thought to be " out of politics," only three issues divided the parties—and Lincoln in his seventy-word speech had backed Clay on each of them. The first was the National Bank, whose new charter had just been vetoed by Jackson. This Bank was not a government monopoly; but it was the caretaker of the

Government's funds—and it could issue paper money to be redeemed in gold or silver on demand. Unhappily, each of the States could also charter banks and these banks could also issue paper money on whatever conditions the State chose to demand—and sometimes the conditions were farcical.

The banking system of the United States was thus anarchic and grossly unfair. Workmen complained that they were paid in the depreciated or worthless notes of irresponsible banks. This was not the fault of the National Bank. Nevertheless that bank, the most important in the nation, had large powers to expand or contract the currency. It became a political football. So when the President vetoed a new charter the opposition became the champions of the Bank. It was not a question of right and wrong, but merely of " ins " and " outs."

The second issue—internal improvements at national expense—involved the theory of federalism: did the central government have the right to use taxes taken from all the people to improve the living conditions in a favoured (or needy) region? The Democrats, under the influence of their godfather Thomas Jefferson, had always been inclined to say " No." So the Whigs said " Yes."

Lincoln's third issue, the protective tariff, was a regional problem. In 1832 it threatened to split the Union. New England and Pennsylvania were already industrialised, and the new factories had begun to creep into the Middle West. The wealth of the South, on the other hand, consisted more and more of slave-stocked plantations producing cotton for the ever-growing demands of Lancashire. The South wished, therefore, to buy her goods in the cheapest market, which was England. She did not choose to be compelled to help the high-cost " infant industries " of the North.

In 1833, Henry Clay produced a prodigy of compromise, whereby he settled the problem for nine years and in effect kept America a low tariff country until the Civil War. Nevertheless, he continued to campaign for a moderate protection, for internal improvements (such as roads, canals, and harbours) which could be charged against the customs revenues, and for a National Bank which would make the currency somewhat less chaotic. He called this three-fold plan " The American System." And such became Lincoln's platform throughout most of his political life.

## V

The Democrats in Illinois were not only a majority; they were an intolerant and self-righteous majority. Their motto was: " All Whigs ought to be whipped out of office like dogs out of a meat house." So the wonder is not that Lincoln lost his first election, but that he was successful in the next four. He became minority leader in the lower house of the State legislature.

Like all good Whigs, and all men who put the Union first, Lincoln was unwilling to countenance the savage intolerance of the abolitionists; but unlike most northern Whigs he was unwilling even to *seem* to countenance slavery. When the Democrats in the Illinois legislature passed a resolution attacking abolition societies, Lincoln wished to add that although the preaching of abolition did more harm than good nevertheless slavery was " founded on both injustice and bad policy."

This was typical of his conservatism and his love of truth: he would never force an issue which could possibly be postponed, but he would never pretend to respect what he thought to be disreputable. He wanted no strife with his neighbours. He did not believe that evil could be cured by societies for the reform of other men. But he was confident it could not be cured by pretending it was not there.

During his days as a State legislator Lincoln left New Salem—which unlike its rival in size (Chicago) soon reverted to the prairie and was never seen again until a grateful nation rebuilt it as a memorial to the backwoods boy.

Lincoln had now learned his Blackstone and was licensed as a lawyer. He settled at Springfield, the new State capital—where he was to live for twenty-four years, until he made the last of his many moves, which took him to Washington.[1]

Lincoln arrived at Springfield on a borrowed horse, with seven dollars in his pocket, and most of his possessions in two saddle bags. He walked into Joshua Speed's store and asked hesitantly for credit to buy bedding. Speed, after studying the kindness and gloom on the stranger's face, said that he himself had a very large room

---

[1] Lincoln, remembering his father who was forever pulling up stakes and seeking new land, liked to tell about the farmer who had moved so often that even the chickens could tell when the next move was coming: they walked up and lay down to have their feet tied.

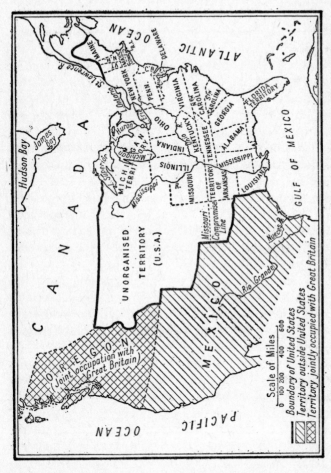

*The United States in 1832, when Lincoln first stood for the State Legislature*

upstairs with a bed big enough for two, and that Lincoln could share it.

This act of charity, this intuition of friendship, was accepted as simply as it was offered. Lincoln took up his saddle-bags and dumped them on the bedroom floor and came down beaming with happiness: " Well, Speed, I'm moved."

He was not only " moved "; he had found a friend for his lonely, reserved spirit. And in Springfield he had reached home: this was where he belonged. Springfield was large enough (it had fifteen hundred people in the 1830's), and important enough politically, to help Lincoln grow steadily in his deliberate way. He had escaped from the backwoods; he had escaped from the tiny village where he studied and pondered and matured. He had now become a small-town lawyer, a small-town politician, which was what he needed and wanted.

There was enough social life in Springfield to smooth his rough edges as much as necessary; yet the little State capital was still part of the prairies which surrounded it, so there was no pressure to remake him into the likeness of metropolitan man, and no lack of bantering appreciation for his odd raw ways of behaving.

Here he could develop his mind and spirit in his own fashion, growing very strong very slowly like the great forests which had surrounded his youth. Whether he would then be needed beyond the parish, beyond the neighbouring counties of his legal circuit, was for destiny to determine. But if the Lord had in fact " called him," he would be ready.

When he left Springfield for the last time, on his way

to the White House, Lincoln spoke from the platform of his railway car: ". . . To this place, and the kindness of these people, I owe everything. Here I have lived for a quarter of a century and have passed from a young to an old man. Here my children have been born and one is buried. I now leave, not knowing when or whether I may return, with a task before me greater than that which rested upon Washington. . . ." Springfield had indeed been his true, his only, home—although he did not find it until the age of twenty-eight.

VI

We have said that Lincoln had little time for women in his eccentric life. His mother was a vague memory of sweetness, and he loved his stepmother; but aside from the doubtful romance with Ann Rutledge his dealings with women of his own age had been awkward, self-conscious, uncomfortable. Yet soon after he settled in Springfield he found himself drawn to Miss Mary Todd, whose father was President of the Lexington Branch of the Bank of Kentucky, and who was visiting her married sister at the Illinois capital.

Miss Todd was handsome, decisive, strong-tempered. She had been born to a life of culture and minor affluence. She is said to have told her friends that she was looking for a husband who would become President of the United States. If she chose Lincoln on such grounds she must have been clairvoyant.

The brilliant, successful Stephen A. Douglas (the "Little Giant" of the Democratic Party who was later to engage Lincoln in the most famous debates in American history, who was to defeat Lincoln for the Senate and to be defeated by him for the presidency) was one of Miss Todd's admirers at Springfield. Yet she preferred the uncouth rail-splitter, and before long she was engaged to marry him.

At once Lincoln plunged into a hell of indecision. Honour, distrust, desire, morbid fear: each seemed to master him successively. His friends feared he might not recover from this attack of nerves. He is said to have tried to break the engagement but to have surrendered before the tears of his betrothed.

Lincoln has been the subject of so much myth-making that we cannot separate truth from fiction in the story of his marriage. Herndon claims that the wedding was first set for January 1841, and that the bridegroom ran away without even an apology or a forewarning. Recent historians deny the tale, though they admit a distressful series of breaks and reconciliations. In any case, the troubled lovers were finally married on November 4th, 1842.

The marriage has caused almost as much gossip as the engagement; but if we stick to the few known facts we must conclude that a great deal of nonsense has been written about Mrs. Lincoln. She was subject to fits of temper which passed the bounds of eccentricity. On the other hand she was a gently reared woman, married to one of the most untidy, careless, unconventional and moody of men. Lincoln never could make himself look like other men, or make a room which he had inhabited for a few hours look like other rooms. Disorder and physical confusion attended him like a shadow. And although it is a virtue to think deeply, prolonged and impenetrable silences in the home do not make for married ease.

Lincoln seems also to have been mildly sardonic towards the niceties, the sense of social dignity, which his wife brought with her from Kentucky.[1] Asked about the spelling of her family name, he replied: "One 'd' is enough for God, but the Todds need two." And he once praised a long-trained dress, of which Mary Lincoln was proud, by walking round her and exclaiming "Whew, what a long tail our cat has!"

There must indeed have been black days and months in any intimate relationship with Lincoln. Yet he and his wife built a true marriage, about which it is not our privilege to invent stories. They had four sons, born between 1843 and 1853. One died at the age of four, one in the White House, and one a few years after Lincoln was murdered. The eldest, Robert Todd Lincoln, lived a long and successful life, but was survived only by daughters.

## VII

Four years after his marriage Lincoln made his first attempt at national politics. He was elected to the House of Representatives in Washington. During the campaign some friends raised a fund of $200 for his

---

[1] "In eating, sleeping, reading, conversation, study," said Joshua Speed, "he was regularly irregular, with no stated time for eating, no fixed time for going to bed, none for getting up."

personal expenses. After the election he sent them back $199.25. " I did not need the money," he said. " I made the canvas on my own horse; my entertainment, being at the houses of friends, cost me nothing; and my only outlay was 75 cents for a barrel of cider, which some farmhands insisted I should treat them to."

In 1847, when Lincoln began his new job, wise men already knew that the slave question had not been put permanently to rest by Clay's Missouri Compromise. Ever since 1836 the enormous State of Texas, which had fought itself free from Mexico, had been asking to join the Union. Texas was slave-territory. It was so large that it might be divided into five or six states, thus upsetting the balance between North and South. Yet if Texas were cold-shouldered she might accept the French and British offer of an alliance—hampering most grievously the westward expansion of the United States. For beyond Texas lay the still vaster lands of New Mexico, California, and Oregon, which most Americans were bent on taking sooner or later, by treaty or by force.[1]

By 1845, therefore, America had to face three fiery questions: Was the slave-system to expand, south of the Missouri Compromise line, as the nation itself expanded? Or was slavery to be allowed in all the new territories, north and south? Or was slavery to be forbidden in every part of the Union where it was not already permitted in 1820?

---

[1] In 1844 France and England offered to guarantee the independence and boundaries of Mexico and Texas. In mad self-assurance Mexico refused—for she would not admit the independence of Texas. The following year Texas joined the Union.

Little by little, as the will to push west to the Pacific became obvious, public opinion hardened on sectional lines. Moral absolutes were proclaimed. Compromise (the price of a federal Union) was condemned. Northern extremists demanded that slavery should never have permission to expand. Southern extremists swore they would secede if they were not granted, at the very least, an extension of the Missouri Compromise line to the western ocean. Between them stood the perplexed but preponderant middle group whose members loved the Union above all else, hated to see slavery reborn as a fighting issue, and were prepared for one last effort to ward off disaster by political concessions. To this group Lincoln belonged.

When he took his seat in Congress, Texas had been received into the American Union; the Oregon Territory had been divided by treaty with Great Britain; the war with Mexico, for all her remaining lands between Texas and Oregon, was under way. This was a war which the United States would gladly forget.

Since the late eighteenth century, first under Spanish and then under Mexican rule, the Californians had been selling hide to Yankee merchantmen. Meanwhile the shoe-making industry of New England flourished and the trade in hides became steadily more profitable.

California was underpopulated and underdeveloped. The Mexican duties were from eighty to a hundred per cent. President Polk (1845-49) knew that with a little bribery and a few threats the Californians could be induced to revolt and to seek American protection. But between Texas and California lay seven hundred miles of Mexican land which must first be acquired by purchase or by war.

Mexico refused to sell—and disobligingly refused to start a war, even after the annexation of Texas. Polk—for all his stubbornness and bigoted contempt towards Mexicans, Whigs, and other adversaries—hesitated to attack with no better excuse than a bare desire to steal some land. Yet what would happen to America's "manifest destiny" if the Mexican empire were not conquered?

Luckily for Polk, Texas had brought with her into the Union a dispute as to her own southern border: the Texans claiming that it was the Rio Grande, the Mexicans that it was the Nueces River which lay farther north. Except in the Texan imagination the Nueces had been the established boundary for a hundred years. President Polk, nevertheless, ordered an American general to take the disputed land and to occupy the bank of the Rio Grande. This led to the desired "incident," in which some American soldiers were killed. Mexico, declared the relieved President, "has invaded our territory and shed American blood upon American soil." This was May 1846. The Congress of the United States promptly declared war.

When Lincoln appeared in Congress the following year, the war had not yet ended; but there was no doubt that the United States would soon annex the provinces of Upper California and New Mexico—a territory which includes the present States of California, Nevada, Utah, Arizona, New Mexico, and parts of Colorado and Wyoming. Yet in spite of the expansion-fever which was now endemic, in spite of the obvious advantage in rounding out the map symmetrically from ocean to ocean, wise men in the North and the South were filled with foreboding. Could the Union survive the harsh struggle over the future of slavery which these conquests must precipitate?

In New England, Ralph Waldo Emerson had warned: " Mexico will poison us." And in the Senate John Caldwell Calhoun, the spokesman for Southern rights, had said, " Mexico is to us the forbidden fruit; the penalty of eating it would be to subject our institutions to political death."

Since Lincoln served only one term in the House of Representatives (1847-49) he did not face at this time the full implications of the new danger. But he had already made clear his unchanging belief about slavery—the belief which later caused him to be hated in the South as a mad radical, to be vilified in the North as a conservative appeaser, but which also caused him to become the saviour of the Union.

" I hold it," Lincoln had written in 1844, " to be the paramount duty of us in the free States, due to the Union of the States, and perhaps to liberty itself (paradox though it may seem) to let the slavery of the other States alone; while, on the other hand, I hold it to be equally clear that we should never knowingly lend ourselves, directly or indirectly, to prevent that slavery from dying a natural death—to find new places for it to live in, when it can no longer exist in the old."

One must marvel at the hysteria which seized the nation during the fifties, causing such cautious views to seem inflammatory. To the abolitionists Lincoln became an immoral trimmer; to the Southern "fire-eaters" he became a potential tyrant. Yet all he said was that no man had a legal right to interfere with slavery in a State where it already existed, and that no man had a moral right " to find new places for it to live in."

Until forced by the break-up of his beloved Union to use the emancipation of slaves as a weapon of war, Lincoln never moved from this view. Yet he was never morally indifferent to the fact of slavery. He sought consistently, stubbornly, even in the midst of the Civil War, to bring about voluntary emancipation, with a cash bonus for those who lost their " property."

In 1849, for example, during his last year in Congress, Lincoln offered a proposal to abolish slavery in the District of Columbia: the sixty square miles which are the seat of the Federal Government and within which the Congress is truly sovereign, with no divided powers. According to Lincoln's plan, compensation was to be paid to the owners of slaves, emancipation was to be gradual, and the act was not to go into force unless the citizens of the District approved it at a special election. On at least two occasions Lincoln voted against bills which would have achieved this end through more radical and rapid steps. Always he preferred the more conservative approach.

By such moderation, by such balance between moral reform and sympathy for man's mistakes, Lincoln might have averted war had he been elected President in 1856 instead of 1860. But in 1856 the misguided politicians were looking for a " safe " President who believed in nothing, who knew nothing about the dark heart of man, and who could be guaranteed to do nothing. They found exactly what they wanted; but the price was high.

## VIII

Unwisely, Lincoln's Whig Party tried to make political capital out of the Mexican War. The war, to be sure, was not a pretty incident; but this is not a pretty world. A war which gains at trivial cost an empire of land (to say nothing of the Californian gold which was promptly found after the annexation) is not likely to be resented by the victors. Statesmen might foresee new sectional strife on the horizon; good men might lament the Bismarckian brutality with which Polk forced the issue; but an adroit political opposition would have let bad enough alone.

In the end the Whigs confessed their folly by nominating for the presidency the most popular general of the war. But at first they insisted that the whole thing was unnecessary and fraudulent. The public was not pleased.

The Whig Senator Corwin of Ohio, for example, was almost asked to resign because of one stirring anti-war speech. Replying to the statement that the nation "needed more room," he said: "This has been the plea of every robber chief from Nimrod to the present hour . . . If I were a Mexican, I would tell you, ' Have you not room in your own country to bury your dead men ? If you come into mine, we will greet you with bloody hands and welcome you to hospitable graves.' "

Abraham Lincoln, meanwhile, kept demanding that

the President indicate the exact spot where the war began, so that citizens could decide for themselves whether the United States had been invaded or had been the aggressor. "As a nation should not, and the Almighty will not, be evaded," said Lincoln, "so let him (the President) attempt no evasion—no equivocation. And if, so answering, he can show that the soil was ours where the first blood of war was shed—then I am with him."

The United States, he explained on a later occasion, was like the land-hungry farmer who said: "I ain't greedy; I only want what jines mine." And he wrote home to the disapproving Herndon: "I will stake my life that if you had been in my place you would have voted just as I did. Would you have voted what you felt and knew to be a lie? I know you would not."

And again: "Allow the President to invade a neighboring nation whenever he shall deem it necessary to repel an invasion . . . and you allow him to make war at pleasure . . . If today he should choose to say he thinks it necessary to invade Canada to prevent the British from invading us, how could you stop him? You may say to him 'I see no probability of the British invading us'; but he will say to you, 'Be silent: I see it, if you don't.' "

These are prophetic words from the man who was himself to revolutionise the office of the presidency by his ruthless use of the "war powers." And in discussing the background of the Mexican War, Lincoln made comments on the theory of revolution which seemed suitable at the time, and exactly in the American tradition, but which were to return to haunt him. "Any people anywhere," he said, " being inclined and having the power, have the right to rise up and shake off the existing government, and form a new one that suits them better . . . Nor is this right confined to cases in which the whole people of an existing government may choose to exercise it. Any portion of such people that can may revolutionize and make their own so much of the territory as they inhabit."

If Lincoln had been seeking to tie his own hands in advance, and to justify the future secession of the South, he could not have done better. Fortunately he had no regard for those who stick stubbornly to their old opinions. " Why, Mr. President, you have changed your mind," said a visitor to the White House. " Yes, I have," said Lincoln, " and I don't think much of a man who isn't wiser today than he was yesterday." This distrust of consistency helped Lincoln to remain humble before the truth.

When a minister said that the Lord was on the side of the North, Lincoln answered: " The Lord is on the the side of the right. It is my constant anxiety and prayer that I and this nation should be on the Lord's side."

In January 1848, as a climax to his opposition to the Mexican War, Lincoln voted for a resolution which referred to that war as " unnecessarily and unconstitutionally begun by the President of the United States." This was going too far. The people of Illinois were not amused. They thought such language unpatriotic, and Lincoln was not sent back to Congress.

The two years in Washington, however, had been a

boon. The backwoods boy had seen the capital city and had travelled through much of the East. And he had learned at first hand the passions which were released in House and Senate whenever the spread of slavery was mentioned. He said later that he must have voted " Aye " about forty times for the hate-laden Wilmot Proviso—which means that he had already seen the North and South near the brink of war. In writing this letter to a friend, Lincoln was indulging in hyperbole. In fact he voted for the principle of the Proviso five times.

As early as 1846, Representative Wilmot of Pennsylvania had begun attaching to various bills an amendment which said that no territory ever acquired from Mexico should be open to slavery. This " Proviso " frequently passed the House, but was always defeated in the Senate. Most men agreed that if it were accepted by both chambers, and if the President signed the bill containing it, secession would result.

In 1847, when the Proviso had been introduced for the second time, President Polk wrote in his diary that it " will be attended with terrible consequences to the country, and cannot fail to destroy the Democratic Party, if it does not ultimately threaten the Union itself." During a later discussion of the same amendment, two Union-loving Representatives from Georgia gave sterner warning. They had been opposed to the Mexican adventure, and to expansion in general; but once the expansion was a fact they must feel the South to be dishonoured if she was not free to take her " peculiar institution " into some part of the new public domain.

" Appropriate this common property to yourselves,"

said Robert Toombs, " it is then your government, not
mine. Then I am its enemy, and I will, if I can, bring
my children and my constituents to the altar of liberty,
and like Hamilcar I would swear them to eternal hostility
to your foul domination." And Alexander Stephens,
who was soon to be Vice-President of the Confederacy,
said that if the Proviso passed, the result would be
" desolation, carnage and blood." These were the
relatively moderate Southerners.

We shall see that the Proviso was at last shelved, and
its evil influence briefly overcome, by a compromise
which took advantage of the obvious fact that climate
excluded slavery from the dry and desolate land between
Texas and California. Thus, by " permitting " slavery
where nature prevented it, Southern honour was satisfied,
and so was Northern insistence that slavery should not
spread.

The mature Lincoln of the late 1850's would have
sought some such device from the beginning. No one
was ever more willing to save his opponent's " face," to
soften defeat by chivalry. He would fight when necessary; if the chance offered he would avoid force and win
by guile; but he would not humiliate his neighbour.
In his great days he came close to combining the wisdom
of the serpent and of the saint.

Meanwhile, his tour of duty at Washington had at
least taught Lincoln the cruelty of politics. When he
was rash and unstatesmanlike (voting five times for an
amendment which was an insult and which was not even
necessary) he found himself popular. When he did
what he knew to be right he failed of renomination.

And while learning to hope for no rewards, and to fear no punishments, Lincoln was also sharpening his powers of debate. Against formidable opponents he discovered how to make himself feared. He did not copy other men's style; but he refined his own, which was to become the best in America for attack or for exposition, but which in 1849 was still rough.

## IX

Lincoln returned to Illinois as a respected member of the minority Whig Party: a State-wide figure, although still unknown nationally. For the next five years he gave himself chiefly to the law. His slow, careful, tenacious mind—his power to think a problem to an exact conclusion and then to dramatise it with some strange tale from the woods or from village life—made him a leader of the Illinois bar. In the legal profession as in all else he had moved gradually but steadily towards his aim. " Of the hustling spirit which the frontier engendered," writes Allan Nevins, " he showed very little; he loved the people about him too much to like combat or self-assertion." [1]

One reason why Lincoln was a wise counsel, and why he learned much from his study of the law, was that he knew by inner grace that mankind does not divide into good people and bad people. " In his own mind," wrote Carl Sandburg, " he made the note: ' The true rule in determining to embrace or reject anything, is not whether it have any evil in it, but whether it have more of

[1] *The Emergence of Lincoln*, vol. 1, p. 356.

evil than of good. Almost everything is an inseparable compound of the two; so that our best judgment of the preponderance between them is continually demanded.' "

Here is the root of wisdom in government and in law. The whole of life is " an inseparable compound " of the better and the worse. Knowing this, Lincoln knew that many ills are inevitable. When he was attacked as a fomenter of discord for saying that the Union could not survive half-slave and half-free, he answered: " I did not express my wish on anything. I simply expressed my expectation. Cannot Judge Douglas perceive a distinction between a purpose and an expectation? I have often expressed an expectation to die, but I have never expressed a wish to die."

Another reason for Lincoln's pre-eminence at the law —in Illinois, where it was still relatively simple, human, and informal—was the pleasure he took in the companionship which his circuit-practice brought him. Three months in the spring and three in the autumn Lincoln toured the Eighth Circuit: fourteen counties in the centre of the State. As he rode on horseback or drove his open buggy across the lonely prairie he had time for the long thoughts which ever since his childhood had possessed him.

And when he reached the rough village tavern at close of day he delighted his fellow lawyers with uncouth stories which were as human as *Æsop's Fables* and as broadly farcical as the *Arabian Nights*. His friendliness and lack of pretension made him loved everywhere. His humour made him a legend throughout the State. " The beauty of his character," said Joshua Speed, " was

its entire simplicity.   He had no affectation in anything. .
When he was ignorant on any subject, no matter how
simple it might make him appear, he was always willing
to acknowledge it."

Yet in spite of his humanity, his homely warmth, he
remained reserved, withdrawn.   " Everybody knew him
and nobody knew him," wrote Sandburg: " He seemed
to have more secrets about himself, that he kept to himself,
than any one else in Illinois.   ' The most secretive shut-
mouthed man I ever saw, or expect to see,' said Judge
David Davis, in whose court Lincoln practised twelve
years.   ' I doubt whether he ever asked anybody's advice
about anything,' said Leonard Swett." [1]

A symbolic picture of Lincoln would show a tall,
sombre, solitary rider, lost in thought, crossing the
endless plain.

[1] *The Prairie Years*, vol. ii, p. 307.

# * 2 *
## Prairie Politics and Law
### 1850-1860

THE COMPROMISE of 1850 was the last national crisis of his lifetime in which Lincoln was not an important figure. Yet it set the stage for his career. His erstwhile hero, Henry Clay—whom he had found disappointingly cold and selfish in later years, but to whom he still referred as " my beau ideal of a statesman "—was the leader of this final effort to ward off secession by political good sense. The motive, once again, was a Lincolnian love for the Union.

Calhoun of South Carolina, unyielding as ever, had countered the Wilmot Proviso with a proposition equally extreme, equally untenable. He said the Congress had no right to prohibit slavery in the public domain, since slaves were common law property and since government was created to protect the property of its citizens, not to abolish it. This doctrine, if accepted, would annul the Missouri Compromise of 1820 (which prohibited slavery in the then existing territories north of 36° 30').

No Northern State would ever consent; but Calhoun welcomed disagreement. He wanted the South to secede immediately, if she could not have her way. before the balance of power between the regions became too unfavourable. The only " concession " he would offer was a constitutional amendment whereby each section would be given the right to veto all Federal laws which did not suit its interest—thus bringing government to a standstill.

If the discussion had remained on this unrealistic plane—a debate between the friends of the Wilmot Proviso and the friends of Calhoun—the unbending Southerner must have forced the issue to the breaking-point. Secession would have come to pass in 1850, before the North could resist. But at the height of the crisis Henry Clay returned to the Senate to make his greatest effort to save the spirit of federalism, which is itself a form of compromise.

Clay, as we have seen, had been in and out of Congress ever since 1810. He had three times sought the presidency and had served as Secretary of State under John Quincy Adams (1825-29). A Virginian by birth, with the charm and expansiveness of the old South, he had grown up with the first of many American " Wests " in Kentucky. Popular, gregarious, emotionally patriotic, he believed himself to have saved the Union in 1820, and again with his tariff compromise in 1833. He was seventy-three in 1850 when he set himself to save it for a third time.

Clay knew that the cotton kingdom, and with it the slave-plantation, could not live west of the 98th meridian, where the Great Plains begin and where the rainfall drops to less than twenty inches and sometimes to less than ten. The whole of the new land taken from

Mexico lay west of ninety-eight. All of it was arid—except the Pacific slopes of the Sierra Nevada, almost within sight of the ocean.

And Clay knew that California, blessed by those bountiful slopes where slavery might flourish, wished to join the Union as a free State. So he saw a chance to propitiate both Southern honour and Northern principles.

In January 1850 he put before the Senate a group of resolutions which made concessions to both sides. First, California was to be admitted with a constitution which forbade slavery. Second, the slave trade in the District of Columbia was to be abolished. Third, the rest of the old Mexican empire was to be organised into territories (Utah and New Mexico), with no provision for or against slavery. Fourth, a more stringent Fugitive Slave Law was to be passed—so that Southerners could no longer complain that their property was seduced by abolitionists into running away.

Two prizes for the North, two for the South—although one of the latter was a prize in name only. Defending his plan in a series of importunate speeches, Clay warned the North that it must take account of Southern pride and fear, that the essence of statesmanship was not to press for the form (which was the Wilmot Proviso) but to accept the substance (which was the impossibility of slavery in the dry cattle country).

And Clay warned the South that secession must mean war—" furious, bloody, implacable, exterminating." He predicted truly that the men of the Middle West, of the upper Mississippi valley, would fight rather than see the mouth of their river in the hands of a foreign power. He made these clear and simple points in speech after speech, week after week: persuasive, ingratiating, eloquent.

Calhoun replied that Clay's measures did not meet the Southern grievances. The South had been deprived, by such acts as the Missouri Compromise, of her natural right to expand. She also lived under the threat that Northern majorities might reimpose a high tariff, which would help only the industrial States and harm only the agricultural. And now she suffered an ever-mounting abuse from abolitionists and other anti-slavery cranks who sought to upset her social system. She must be given the power to veto Federal laws, or she must secede.

If no such veto power could be granted, Calhoun doubtless preferred an immediate break. But the majority of Southerners still wanted the Union, still longed for compromise. Under the leadership of men like Toombs and Stephens of Georgia the South was ready to support Clay—if the North would accept all four of his proposals. The debate in the Senate centred on the new and cruel Fugitive Slave Law—for which only Senator Daniel Webster of Massachusetts could hope to win the necessary Northern votes.

Webster was the third of the elder statesmen who had dominated the Congress for forty years. Like the others he was now to make his last important appearance. He did not rely upon affection, like Clay, or upon logic like Calhoun, but upon the impressiveness of his presence. Carlyle wrote of his " crag-like face; the dull black eyes under the precipice of brows, like dull anthracite furnaces, needing only to be *blown*; the mastiff mouth accurately closed."

When Webster rose to debate Clay's plan, on the seventh of March, 1850, his audience knew that New England's men of letters were ready to revile him in prose and verse if he dared defend the Fugitive Slave Act —and so were most of the younger politicians in the North, who were impatient to inherit his leadership. Webster's first words were thus doubly dramatic: " I speak today for the preservation of the Union. Hear me for my cause."

The full force of Webster's legendary personality was put behind Clay's measures. In the past he had often trimmed, often changed sides for personal advantages; but on that famous seventh of March he spoke for peace, implored the Senate for high-mindedness. " No speech more patriotic or evincing a higher degree of moral courage had ever been made in Congress," writes Allan Nevins. " For once Webster rose to the height of statesmanship. In the fierce light of the history written by events during the next generation, hardly a line of his address failed to meet the test of truth and wisdom."[1] Yet Ralph Waldo Emerson remarked : " The word honour in the mouth of Mr. Webster is like the word love in the mouth of a whore." This is the type of hysteria that drove the nation to war.

The Compromise was accepted in September 1850. By that time Calhoun was dead. Clay and Webster were soon to follow him to the grave. If the younger generation, which then took the stage, had acted in the spirit of these two men, the settlement of 1850 might have been decisive. The moderates could have kept power in the

[1] *Ordeal of the Union*, vol. i, pp. 290-1.

South. The Union could have been saved without war. And Lincoln might have remained a country lawyer. But the ruthless breaking of the Compromise within four years called Lincoln back into politics and made him the essential spokesman for all that was best in the Union.

## II

During the presidential election of 1852 both major parties praised the Compromise. A number of Southern Whigs, however, thought that their candidate, General Scott, was too Northern in his ideas; so they joined the Democratic Party, whose candidate had no ideas at all. And a number of Northern Whigs thought that poor General Scott was the tool of the " slave-power "; so they formed a dissenting party which proclaimed " that the Fugitive Slave Act is repugnant to the Constitution, to the principles of the common law, to the spirit of Christianity, and to the sentiments of the civilized world." They polled only 150,000 votes. And a party of Southern " fire-eaters," preaching secession, polled only 3,500.

The country had chosen harmony and had asked for a rest from name-calling. But such blessings are not attained by spinelessness. Unhappily, the Democratic Party had named Franklin Pierce for President: one of the weakest and most aimless of men. He was elected because he had no enemies—and as often happens in such cases he also had no friends, no character, no fixed principles. Yet he easily won the election.

By the time Pierce was inaugurated, in 1853, contentious men in both regions were set to ruin the Compromise: some for personal advancement, and others because they were such babies in politics that they did not know this was the last chance for peace. Ralph Waldo Emerson was an example of the second type. He declared private war on the Fugitive Slave Act, saying it was a law " which no man can obey, or abet the obeying, without loss of self-respect and forfeiture of the name of a gentleman."

Emerson was following good American precedent in deciding for himself which laws to obey, and which to disregard on the ground that they were immoral and therefore void. Yet this is a dangerous game when the stakes are the life of a nation.

If Emerson had understood that a large federal democracy lives by mutual concessions and not by priggishness, he might have softened his language. Or perhaps it was too late. Perhaps, in Lincoln's words, it was already time to say of the gathering civil strife—not between good men and bad, but between perplexed, misguided brothers—that " if God wills that it continue until all the wealth piled up by the bondsman's two hundred and fifty years of unrequited toil shall be sunk, and until every drop of blood drawn with the lash shall be paid by another drawn with the sword, as was said three thousand years ago, so still it must be said ' The judgments of the Lord are true and righteous altogether.' "

Or in the words of " The Battle Hymn of the Republic " (1862):

*He has sounded forth the trumpets that shall never call retreat;*
*He is sifting out the hearts of men before His judgment seat:*
*Oh! be swift, my soul, to answer Him! be jubilant, my feet!*

Perhaps it was indeed too late, even in 1853. But the politician should never admit such pessimism, should never be " jubilant " at the thought that politics have failed and that the sword must intervene. Lincoln's words, quoted above, are taken from his Second Inaugural Address—towards the end of the war which he had done all that man might do to make unnecessary. If President Pierce (1853-57) or President Buchanan (1857-61) had possessed a tithe of Lincoln's persistence and wisdom, the tragic tension might have been resolved. Politics is the art of making the best of a bad business— admitting that we shall never make earth a heaven, but insisting that we must not make it a hell.

All this was a closed book to Franklin Pierce. He had been chosen to do nothing—chosen by men who forgot that " nothing " may be the equivalent of death. A better man could at least have united the large majority which wished to give the Compromise a chance, so that hysteria might diminish. The nation would have gained time to try to abolish slavery gradually, on Lincoln's lines, with compensation to the owners and with honour between North and South.

But Pierce, as was intended by his backers, lacked the character to insist that the Compromise of 1850 must now be taken as irrevocable. So the nation was soon plunged into hatreds deeper than those born of the Wilmot Proviso—the excuse for the reopening of the

wound being the question of whether Chicago or New
Orleans should get rich first, of whether the Northern
or Southern economy should first profit from the new
West.

## III

The time had come for a transcontinental railway in
the United States. Should it run from New Orleans to
Vicksburg, and then through Texas and New Mexico to
Los Angeles? Or should it run from Chicago, through
Nebraska and Salt Lake City to San Francisco? Jefferson
Davis of Mississippi, who had been Lincoln's childhood
neighbour in Kentucky and who was now Secretary of
War in Pierce's Cabinet, backed the former route. Senator
Stephen A. Douglas of Illinois (the former suitor of Mary
Todd Lincoln) backed the latter. They were both
Democrats, and since the Whigs had begun to disintegrate
in 1852 the Democratic Party was the strongest link
between the regions: a federal union within itself. That
Union was now to be endangered for the sake of sectional
ambitions. The one man who might have intervened
was the President of the United States, who alone represented the nation as a whole. But he did what he had
been nominated to do: an amiable nothing.

If the road was to run west from Chicago (which was
no longer in the New Salem class, but which in 1850
was still a village), the first step was to create a territorial government in the wild unsettled land north and
west of Missouri, which was vaguely known as Nebraska.
Naturally, therefore, the Southern members of Congress

blocked every attempt to organise Nebraska—until Senator Douglas devised a scheme to lure them to his support. In January 1854, he introduced a bill which repealed the Missouri Compromise and abolished the old agreement that slavery should not spread north of 36° 30'.

The bill authorised two new territories: Nebraska and Kansas. The settlers were to decide the question of slavery for themselves, on the principle of "popular sovereignty." As we have seen, Utah and New Mexico had already been organised on this basis—but only because the North knew that plantation-agriculture could not live in that dry country. But now—to win Southern votes for his Chicago-railway plan—Douglas proposed the same system for lands where slave-based farms might flourish.

The Southerners took the bait. They induced the President to put the power of the Administration behind the Kansas-Nebraska Act, behind the repeal of the Missouri Compromise. In this they gravely mistook the North—as did Stephen A. Douglas, who was reputed to be the wiliest of politicians.

" It is impossible for such a man," writes Allan Nevins, " to comprehend the fervent emotion with which millions of freedom-loving Northerners regarded the possibility that half the great West might become a land of slaves . . . When indignation welled up like the ocean lashed by a hurricane he was amazed. The fact that the irresistible tidal forces in history are moral forces always escapes a man of dim moral perceptions." [1]

[1] *Ordeal of the Union*, vol. ii, pp. 107-8.

Douglas was burnt in effigy throughout the Northern states. Anti-Nebraska groups—soon to coalesce into the new Republican Party—were formed in every village church and court-house north of the Ohio River. Yet Douglas, backed by the party machine, forced the Kansas-Nebraska Act through Congress. As he had hoped and planned, when the first transcontinental railway was completed the eastern terminus was Chicago. But even the real-estate speculators in that soon-to-be-opulent town might have shuddered if they had foreseen in 1854 the price which all this trickery would exact.

Douglas received a hint of what was in store when he returned to Illinois from his congressional triumph to answer the attacks of Abraham Lincoln, whose long years of silent preparation were now ended. The man and the occasion had at last met.

The nation did not want oratory and abuse—Congress had abounded in both during the fiery Kansas-Nebraska debates. It wanted a simple, homely, conservative but moral explanation as to why this thing was wrong, as to where the free States must make a final stand. Above all it wanted an explanation which was humble and human, not a self-righteous tale of good men and demons. The whole of Lincoln's life had been a preparation for this task. Once he assumed the burden he was never to lay it down.

Twice in the month of October 1854 Lincoln told his Illinois neighbours why Douglas's plan was callous and morally wrong. " I think I have no prejudice against the Southern people," he said. " They are just what we would be in their situation. If slavery did not now exist among them, they would not introduce it. If it did now exist among us, we should not instantly give it up. . . . If all earthly power were given me, I should not know what to do, as to the existing institution. . . . But all this, to my judgment, furnishes no more excuse for permitting slavery to go into our free territory, than it would for reviving the African slave trade by law. . . .

"But Nebraska is urged as a great Union-saving measure. Well, I too go for saving the Union. . . . But I must believe, at least, that the means I employ have some adaptation to the end. To my mind, Nebraska has no such adaptation. ' It hath no relish of salvation in it.' It is an aggravation, rather, of the only one thing which ever endangers the Union. . . . In the whole range of possibility, there scarcely appears to me to have been anything, out of which the slavery agitation could have been revived, except the very project of repealing the Missouri Compromise. . . . Repeal the Missouri Compromise—repeal all compromises—repeal the Declaration of Independence—repeal all past history, you still cannot repeal human nature. It will still be the abundance of man's heart that slavery extension is wrong; and out of the abundance of his heart, his mouth will continue to speak. . . .

" In his " (Senator Douglas's) " view, the question of whether a new country shall be slave or free is a matter of as utter indifference as it is whether his neighbour shall plant his farm with tobacco or stock it with horned cattle. . . . The great mass of mankind take a totally different view. They consider slavery a great moral wrong; and their feeling against it is not evanescent, but eternal. It lies at the very foundation of their sense of justice, and it cannot be trifled with."

This is the new note for which men had been waiting. This transcends Emerson's loose abuse of Southerners as " barbarians." We are reminded of Sandburg's statement that Lincoln talked to an audience as if he were exchanging thoughts with a friend while driving across the prairies. He had no easy answers, and above all no smugness; but he knew that the spread of slavery was wrong and that most men agreed in their hearts. He knew that some truths are indeed eternal, built into the structure of the world, and that no legislature can repeal them.

Faith in a natural law is the rock on which the nation had been founded. It is affirmed in the preamble to the Declaration of Independence, which Lincoln said was the source of all his politics. It is a faith which makes some men arrogant, for they identify the law of nature with their own daily prejudices; but it made Lincoln humble. All his life he sought to discover that law and to serve it.

## IV

The first and inevitable result of the Nebraska bill was " Bleeding Kansas." Nebraska was too far north for the slave-owners to hope to settle it. The moment it was opened, free farmers flooded in. Popular sovereignty, in the absence of a large dissenting group, worked as smoothly as Douglas had predicted. But Kansas lay due west of Missouri, a slave State. What was the point of Douglas's "concession" to Jefferson Davis and his friends, if the South were to take no advantage of her new permission to move the "peculiar institution" beyond the old line?

Kansas was doomed to become a minor battlefield. The South sought to seize it for herself. The North hurried to fill the region with free men, so that they might out-vote the Southerners when the time came to decide the question of slavery. In far-off New England, societies were formed to finance migration. And in Kansas the two groups eyed each other sullenly, each preparing to resist an adverse vote by fraud or by force.

Since the slave-owning Missourians lived next door, they got there first with the most voters and won the early elections. But the results were rejected by the free settlers and by Northern public opinion. Later, therefore, when Northern wealth and numbers had done their work and the anti-slavery men had a majority, Southern members of Congress refused to let Kansas enter the Union as a free State. Finally, the two groups within that unhappy territory began burning each other's home-steads—and with the advent of the God-intoxicated John Brown they advanced from arson to murder.

If a peaceful decision had ever been possible in Kansas, if Douglas's plan had not been wholly unrealistic in view of the popular passions, there is no doubt what the decision would have been. The North had not only the men and the money: it was now building the railways which were to link the new North-west (across the Mississippi) with the Middle West and the North-east. The rivers which drained into the Mississippi and thus into the Gulf of Mexico had for generations diverted the commerce of the vast central valley towards the South. But the railways, running east and west, now took that commerce far more quickly to the markets of the world. Chicago had by 1856 become the traffic centre for a new empire. " The parallels had conquered the meridian lines of comerce." [1]

If " popular sovereignty " had been faithfully applied, Kansas would soon have become a free territory. But the South refused the verdict of the ballot box. She claimed she had been promised a new outlet for slavery —and now the promise was being withdrawn.

At one election for a territorial legislature in Kansas, 1,266 pro-slavery ballots were cast in a county which had less than a hundred voters. A village on the Missouri line which contained half a dozen houses cast 1,628 votes. Soon thereafter a convention (which according to the Emporia *News* was packed with " broken-down political hacks, demagogues, fire-eaters, perjurers, ruffians, ballot-box stuffers, and loafers ") adopted a constitution which declared slave property inviolable. The voters were allowed to take the constitution with or without that article; but even if they rejected the article there could be no interference with the slaves already in Kansas.

Under such conditions words like " democracy " or " popular sovereignty " became a joke. The nation slipped farther and farther into hysteria. The North truly believed that the " slave-power," having seized Kansas, would divide Texas into five or six States, annex Mexico and Cuba, and impose its hateful system upon the

[1] Allan Nevins, *Ordeal of the Union*, vol. ii, p. 227.

new North-west. The South truly believed that the
ridiculous Kansas Convention had been legally elected,
and had made a proper constitution, and that Congress
should at once accept Kansas as a slave State. " The
true issue," said the half-brother of Alexander Stephens,
" is . . . whether a State with slavery is fit to be admitted
into the Union. If it be decided against us honor leaves
us but one course, and that is, for all the slave States to
walk out of the Union, and fling their defiance behind
them; and if no other will, I hope Georgia will do it,
solitary and alone."

Meanwhile, each new outrage in " Bleeding Kansas "
increased the bitterness of congressional speeches, congressional passions. Members of the national legislature
were beginning to treat each other like delegates from
hostile powers. The fateful repeal of the Missouri
Compromise was producing all the woe which Lincoln
had predicted. It also, unexpectedly, produced the new
political party which was soon to make Lincoln President.

## V

We have seen that the Whig Party was disintegrating in
1852. It was bound to go down with the great Compromise which it had fathered but which it had failed to
protect. When the old hatreds were revived by Kansas-
Nebraska the Whigs had nothing left to suggest. Their
two great leaders, Henry Clay and Daniel Webster,
were dead. Their last magnanimous plan to save the
Union was also dead—although it had at least post-
poned secession, so that when the sword was finally

*Plate 4.   The last portrait, taken four days before Lincoln's death*
from Stefan Lorant's
'Lincoln, A Picture Story of His Life'

# AMERICA.

# ASSASSINATION
## OF
# PRESIDENT
# L·I N C O L N.

## ATTEMPTED MURDER OF
## MR. SEWARD..

(REUTER'S TELEGRAMS.)

NEW YORK, APRIL 15 (10 A.M.).

At 1.30 this morning Mr. Stanton reported as follows :—

"This evening, at 9.30, President Lincoln, while sitting in a private box at Ford's theatre with Mrs. Lincoln, Mrs. Harris, and Major Rathburn, was shot by an assassin, who suddenly entered the box, and approached behind the President. The assassin then leaped upon the stage, brandishing a large knife and escaped in the rear of the theatre. A pistol ball entered the back of the President's head, penetrating nearly through. The wound is mortal.

"The President has been insensible ever since the infliction of the wound, and is now dying.

"About the same hour an assassin, whether

*Plate 5. Reuters' scoop report of Lincoln's assassination*

drawn the impetuous valour of the Confederacy could no longer prevail.

Throughout the fifties the Whigs kept murmuring feebly, ineffectually, about " Union " and " patriotism." Their Southern members thought this was a Yankee trick and deserted to the Democratic Party. Their Northern members thought it was a slave-owners' trick and deserted to various " anti " groups: Anti-immigrants, anti-drink, abolitionists, and anti-slavery-in-the-new-territories. The Kansas-Nebraska Act gave Northern politicians a chance to collect these heterogeneous objectors into a new and powerful party: a party which had to be sectional in membership (since no Southerner would touch it), but which was national in policy, and which drew its votes from the region where the majority lived.

The same week that the Nebraska bill appeared before the Senate, a meeting was held in Wisconsin to launch a political party " on the sole basis of the non-extension of slavery." Like most American radicals the founders of this movement claimed to be descended from Thomas Jefferson, who had striven stubbornly to remove the curse of slavery from his beloved state of Virginia. Therefore they called themselves the Republican Party, which was the name first used by Jefferson. Within a few months, conventions in Michigan, Indiana, Ohio and Vermont had adopted the name and endorsed the programme.

This was a good beginning; but if Republicans were to win national elections they would need a more widely seductive programme than " the non-extension of

E

slavery." Neither the tradesmen of New York and Boston (who were tied commercially to the South), nor the manufacturers of Pennsylvania (who were fanatically protectionist), would support an upstart, regional party unless the party promised to support them.

The professional touch was needed—and it was supplied by local leaders of the dying Whig Party, who saw themselves looking for jobs unless they could quickly build a new machine. Suddenly it occurred to them that they had an attractive policy ready to hand—a policy which might even make a virtue out of the enforced regionalism of their party.

We have seen that Abraham Lincoln had been a lifelong Whig and that his programme (" short and sweet like the old lady's dance ") was Clay's " American System ": a national bank, a high tariff, and internal improvements at federal expense. But the Southern wing of the Whig Party had never liked this plan and had half-frustrated it. Now, however, the most active Southern Whigs had joined the Democrats. Why, then, should not the Northern Whigs impose their " System " upon the new-born Republicans?

The paper-money chaos remained as absurd as ever —so Northern capital (and much of Northern labour) would welcome a national bank, or at least a sound money system under effective national control. The manufacturers of Pennsylvania (a " key " State if the Republicans were to win the presidency) were deep in a business depression. They would back any party which offered them a tariff. And as for " internal improvements at federal expense "—why not translate those ambiguous words into land-grants, out of the public domain, for the building of railways by private enterprise? The "federal expense" and the "improvements" would be provided, and also some new rich Republicans.

One further political hunger which might be turned into votes was the hunger for free homesteads in the territories. This, too, the South had frustrated—for fear it would hasten the rise of States hostile to slavery. But a new party, searching for members, could not reject so obvious an attraction. Thus the Republicans espoused free land. "Vote yourself a farm," they said to the labourer who wanted to move West. "Vote yourself a tariff," to the manufacturer who feared British competition. And "vote yourself a stable money-system," to the capitalist class as a whole, and to the factory worker who was tired of being paid with inflated paper.

The one thing needed (when this broad-based programme had been devised and accepted) was a leader who believed in it, and who also believed (with the sincere and simple founders of the Republican Party) that slavery must not spread. Abraham Lincoln would seem to have been born for the job. As a westerner he naturally favoured free land and federal aid to the more backward regions. Henry Clay had taught him long ago to believe in a national bank and a tariff. His views on slavery were exactly right. In addition he was a cautious man of great forbearance, who was never tempted to extremes. The early, indignant, anti-Nebraska Republicans included a number of cranks. If the party was to win the conservative east without losing its western roots and western enthusiasm, it must find a leader who could keep the cranks in line but who would not be swayed by them in policy.

By 1860 the Republican Party had a well-rounded programme which might appeal to all classes and to all the Northern regions; but its whole soul derived from two principles: (that the Union must not be dissolved, and that slavery must not spread into new territories.) Lincoln was the guardian of that soul, against the bitter Left and the soft Right: the abolitionists who so hated the South that they would be glad to force disunion, and the eastern merchants who did such good business with the South (and were owed such large debts by her) that they were ready for appeasement—for a friendly secession which would not interfere with the paying of old bills.

## VI

At the first Republican National Convention, in 1856, Lincoln had received the second largest number of votes for the vice-presidential nomination. Although he had seldom been outside his own State the news was spreading that here was a wise and steady man who had made his odd looks into an asset and who had the rare magic which attracts votes. Two years later—at the age of 49—he at last became a major national figure. By that time the Kansas-Nebraska Act had done its full damage and the Supreme Court had added an almost equivalent folly. The hour of decision was at hand.

In 1857 Pierce had been succeeded in the White House by James Buchanan, another Democrat of infirm will. Buchanan had spent forty years in public life; but he had learned nothing except the gentle art of side-stepping important issues. Behind an appearance of pompous confidence he was self-distrustful and timid. Irresolute in every emergency, he thought the chief task of a leader was to repeat from time to time that nothing was really as bad as it seemed. By such incantations, and by deft political "deals," he hoped to bring quiet to his distracted country. Instead, by his weakness and his Southern bias, he helped create the fatal split within the Democratic Party.

A few days before his inauguration Buchanan was told that the Supreme Court of the United States was about to "settle" the problem of slavery. The Court would announce that the Missouri Compromise was unconstitutional—that Congress had never possessed the power to banish slavery from any part of the public domain! Amazingly, Buchanan believed that these rash and ageing judges could calm the national frenzy. When they had spoken, the ruffians in "Bleeding Kansas" would feel ashamed, and the nation would settle blissfully into a long period of peace. This, at least, is what Buchanan suggested in his Inaugural Address.

Promptly the Supreme Court made the expected decision; but the result was not what Buchanan had foreseen. The case concerned a Negro named Dred Scott, who sued for his freedom on the ground that he had lived for years in a territory which was free under the Missouri Compromise. But since the Court found that Compromise null and void, no one could have become free by living in a territory. A State might outlaw slavery within its own borders; but Congress had no such power in a territory which belonged to the whole nation. " An act of Congress," wrote the Chief Justice, " which deprives a citizen of the United States (i.e. Dred's master) of his liberty or property, merely because he came himself or brought his property into a particular territory of the United States, and who had committed no offence against the laws, could hardly be dignified with the name of due process of law." The Court need not have discussed the Missouri Compromise, for it had already ruled that Dred Scott, a slave, had no constitutional right to sue in a federal court. The inflaming and impolitic material was contained in *obiter dicta*.

The decision was especially interesting to Lincoln, because it made the Republican Party as unconstitutional as the Missouri Compromise. After all, the party's first purpose was to prevent the spread of slavery into new territories. Naturally, Lincoln and his friends took the view that the Court was wrong, and that in time a more sensible Court would reverse the judgment. Meanwhile no legal logic could make the majority of Northern people accept something which they thought abominable. The New York *Tribune*, for example, called the Dred Scott decision " this wicked and false judgment " which was " entitled to just as much moral weight as would be the judgment of a majority of those congregated in any Washington bar-room."

One by one, all the institutions which had given strength to the Union were being undermined. The Whig Party (the party of compromise) had been impatiently deserted by its Northern and Southern members. Pierce and Buchanan had made the presidency into an office of no influence and no decision, and were thereby weakening the Democratic Party as well. Douglas, with his Nebraska Act, had made " popular sovereignty " seem silly, and had caused a new sectional party to arise. And now, in the eyes of the Northern majority, even the Supreme Court had begun to degrade itself.

The one institution which was strengthened by Nebraska and by the Dred Scott decision was the Republican Party; the one national leader who was strengthened was Abraham Lincoln. In this hour of bad tempers and of waning faith, Lincoln's combination of conservatism, generosity, and homely morality went to men's hearts. And the audacious, thrusting Stephen A. Douglas, Democratic senator from Lincoln's own State, proved a perfect foil for showing off such qualities.

## VII

Even in appearance Senator Douglas was designed by Providence as an amusing contrast to Lincoln. Douglas —" the Little Giant "—was five foot tall, with spindly legs, an athlete's chest, a large head, a bull-like neck and an enormous voice. He seemed to burn with energy and restlessness. Headlong, warmly affectionate, but with great natural dignity—his whole life had been a political triumph. He walked and dressed and talked like one who commanded success. He made Lincoln look more than usually odd: tall, gangling, awkward, with a small head and a shrill voice, his clothes absurdly ill-fitting, his stove-pipe hat and his umbrella absurdly old—all of which Lincoln knew, and emphasised, and relished.

Douglas was too wise to underestimate Lincoln. He was in Washington in 1858 when he heard that the Republicans of Illinois had made Lincoln their candidate for the Senate—for Douglas's own job. He said to his friends: " Lincoln is the strong man of his party, full of wit, facts, dates—and the best stump speaker, with his droll ways and dry jokes, in the West."

The two men had recently clashed over the Dred Scott decision, which Douglas had tried to reconcile with his famous doctrine that the people in a territory must decide for themselves about a slavery. Of course, he said, a citizen might take his slaves to a territory; but that was " a barren and worthless right unless sustained, protected, and enforced by appropriate police regulations and local legislation, prescribing adequate remedies for its violation." Thus Dred Scott did not contradict " popular sovereignty." And then Douglas added—for the fun of reminding the Republicans that their whole party had been declared unconstitutional: " Whoever resists the final decision of the highest tribunal aims a deadly blow at our . . . system of government."

The speech was unlucky. The statement that slavery could be kept out of the territories by the refusal of police protection frightened the South and set the " fire-eaters " against Douglas, thus destroying his chances for the presidency in 1860. And the pompous talk about " resisting the highest tribunal " gave Lincoln a chance to discuss (at Douglas's expense) one of the most interesting problems in American politics: who is to decide what the Constitution means?

Must the President and the Congress always bow to

the Supreme Court? Or was President Jackson right when he said in a veto message, " Each public officer, who takes an oath to support the Constitution, swears that he will support it as he understands it, and not as it is understood by others "? (This was a question which Lincoln was to face daily, during his war-darkened years in the White House.)

Douglas had proclaimed that if the Republicans opposed the Dred Scott decision it would " become a distinct and naked issue between the friends and enemies of the Constitution—the friends and enemies of the supremacy of the laws." To this Lincoln gave two answers.

First, he said that the Republicans " think the Dred Scott decision is erroneous. We know that the Court that made it has often overruled its own decisions, and we shall do what we can to have it overrule this. We offer no *resistance* to it." In other words, they planned no revolution. But they did plan to gain the presidency and to appoint Supreme Court Justices whose ideas they deemed more sensible.

Second, he referred to Andrew Jackson's famous veto of the bill to re-charter the National Bank.[1] The Supreme Court had declared the Bank constitutional; yet President Jackson decided that it was not. " Again and again," said Lincoln mildly, " I have heard Judge Douglas denounce that bank decision (of the Supreme Court) and applaud General Jackson for disregarding it. It would be interesting for him to look over his recent speech, and see how exactly his fierce philippics against

[1] Cp. page 27 for the Jackson-Whig controversy over the Bank.

us for resisting Supreme Court decisions fall upon his own head."

And in conclusion Lincoln redefined the meaning, or at any rate the soul, of the Republican Party: "The Republicans inculcate, with whatever ability they can, that the Negro is a man, that his bondage is cruelly wrong, and that the field of his oppression ought not to be enlarged. The Democrats deny his manhood; deny, or dwarf to insignificance the wrong of his bondage; so far as possible, crush all sympathy for him, and cultivate and excite hatred and disgust against him; compliment themselves as Union-savers for doing so; and call the indefinite outspreading of his bondage 'a sacred right of self-government.'

"The plainest print cannot be read through a gold eagle; and it will ever be hard to find many men who will send a slave to Liberia, and pay his passage, while they can send him to a new country—Kansas, for instance, and sell him for fifteen hundred dollars, and the rise."

We can see why Douglas was uneasy when he heard that Lincoln had been chosen to try to oust him from the Senate.[1] It was magnanimous of Douglas, therefore, to accept Lincoln's challenge to debate the issues face to face, up and down the State of Illinois—especially since Lincoln could not command the audiences which would turn out for the "Little Giant." But no man ever accused Douglas of dodging trouble.

[1] United States Senators, in 1858, were still appointed by the state legislatures, not elected by the direct vote of the constituents. Lincoln and Douglas were canvassing for party votes: whichever party won a majority of the Illinois legislature would have the choice of Senator.

Although the Lincoln-Douglas debates of 1858 are the most famous in American history, and are known in outline to every schoolboy in the northern States, the two men added little to what they had already said. Perhaps they were not really very far apart. " He and I are about the best friends in the world," said Lincoln in one of the debates, after the Senator had lost his temper and begun calling names. In regard to slavery, the chief issue between them was whether the opposition to its expansion should be put on moral or on purely legal grounds.

Douglas truly believed—in spite of " Bleeding Kansas " and Dred Scott—that his Nebraska bill had not been a mistake, and that the principle of popular sovereignty would prevent the rise of new slave territories. " I have defended it against the North and the South, and I will defend it against whoever assails it, and I will follow it wherever its logical conclusion leads me."

Lincoln truly believed that popular sovereignty could be upset by mobs or frustrated by judges, and that only by accepting a moral prohibition against the spread of slavery could the perturbation of the Northern peoples be abated and the Union saved. In the last speech of his campaign, following the debates, he put his case with his own matchless clarity:

". . . I have neither assailed nor wrestled with any part of the Constitution. The legal right of the southern people to reclaim their fugitives I have constantly admitted. The legal right of Congress to interfere with their institution in the States I have constantly denied. In resisting the spread of slavery to new territory . . . my whole effort has consisted. To the best of my judgment I have labored *for* and not *against* the Union. As I have not felt, so I have not expressed any harsh sentiments toward our southern brethren. I have constantly declared, as I really believed, the only difference between them and us, is the difference of circumstances. . . .

"Ambition has been ascribed to me. God knows how sincerely I prayed that this field of ambition might not be opened. I claim no insensibility to political honors; but today could the Missouri restriction be restored, and the whole slavery question replaced on the old ground of 'toleration' by *necessity* where it exists, with unyielding hostility to the spread of it, on principle, I would, in consideration, gladly agree that Judge Douglas should never be *out*, and I never *in*, an office, so long as we both or either live."

In the same speech Lincoln spoke sadly about the abuse which had been poured upon him during the campaign. Inveterate rancour was thenceforth to follow him to the end. This tolerant, quiet-spoken, melancholy man was fated to bear on his stooped shoulders the full weight of all the hatreds which an inflamed democracy can engender. He seldom found time to complain; but here at the beginning of his road he showed for a minute how the rough insensitive epithets hurt him. And he added, "I have meant to assail the motives of no party, or individuals; and if I have, in any instance (of which I am not conscious) departed from my purpose, I regret it."

The results of the election were almost a dead heat, Lincoln winning the northern counties of Illinois and Douglas most of the southern. The Republican Party had a small majority of the votes, but because of an unfair apportionment of seats the Democrats still held the legislature. Douglas returned to the Senate—having helped Lincoln to win national renown.

## VIII

The strangest fact about the Lincoln-Douglas debates was the persistence with which both men stuck to the question of slavery. But in truth—although the nation was suffering from an economic depression—there was not much else to discuss. As good Westerners, Lincoln and Douglas both believed in free homesteads and in internal improvements at federal expense—Douglas having been one of the first Senators to propose land grants for railway companies. Neither candidate was much interested in the tariff, which was not a problem in Illinois. Both candidates were overwhelmingly pro-Union. So since they had to argue, they were lucky to find the emotional subject of slavery at their disposal.

And Lincoln, at least, had a second reason for concentrating on the one point. We have seen that his new Republican Party had been put together hurriedly out of conservative Whigs (like himself), and Democrats who had deserted Douglas because of the Nebraska act, and abolitionists whom Lincoln regarded as a danger and a nuisance, and odd little groups who were opposed to whatever their neighbours happened to be doing and who could therefore be assumed to oppose slavery. Such a young and heterogeneous gathering (which had only fought one national election and had little party loyalty) could not be allowed to discuss many subjects: it might easily begin disagreeing with itself.

Later, when the rewards of office were available for a cement, and when the local machinery of the party had been stably founded and had acquired vested interests of its own, the time would come to weed out the more improbable cranks and to wheedle the other groups into accepting a policy which would win the most votes throughout the nation. But in 1858 there was only one idea they all had in common, and which Lincoln had in common with them. So he was wise to talk about nothing else. His job, as he said to a friend, was " to hedge against divisions in the Republican ranks generally, and particularly for the contest of 1860."

This was not an easy job, either in Illinois or throughout the North. Anti-immigrant groups in one State, abolitionists in another, persisted in talking out of turn. Lincoln's hard political sense was outraged. " Massachusetts Republicans," he wrote, " should have looked beyond their noses, and then they could not have failed to see that tilting against foreigners would ruin us in the whole Northwest. New Hampshire and Ohio should forbear tilting against the Fugitive Slave Law in such a way as to utterly overwhelm us in Illinois with the charges of enmity to the Constitution itself." Only men with the tact and patience of Lincoln can hope to piece together a new political party in a huge, diffuse, and argumentative federal empire.

If we turn from Illinois to Washington, where everybody had long since run out of tact and patience, we shall find the Congress fighting fiercely over all the issues which Lincoln and Douglas had been so careful to ignore: the Pacific railway and internal improvements, the Homestead Act, and the tariff.

We have seen that the origin of the ill-fated Nebraska Act lay in a rivalry between Douglas and his Northern friends on the one side, and Jefferson Davis and his Southern friends on the other, as to where the first Pacific railway should be built. Since neither section would give way, men had begun to wonder whether the nation would have to build two or three railways in order to grant itself permission to have one.

Inevitably, when the old debate was resumed after the congressional elections, the question of whether the Union itself was to endure lay behind most of the speeches. In January 1859 Senator Iverson of Georgia put the point bluntly: " I believe that the time will come when the slave States will be compelled, in vindication of their rights, interests, and honor, to separate from the free States and erect an independent confederacy . . . And, sir, it is because I believe that separation is not far distant . . . that I am unwilling to vote so much land and so much money as this bill proposes, to build a railroad to the Pacific, which, in my judgment, will be created outside of a southern confederacy, and will belong exclusively to the North."

Similarly, Northern Senators were not prepared to tax their constituents for the sake of a Southern railway to the Pacific, if the South was about to secede. The deadlock was unbreakable. The whole project was post-poned until after the elections of 1860.

The same was true of the Homestead Act. Eastern Republicans had accepted free land as part of their programme because it was a vote-winner, and in spite of their fear that it might lure too many factory-hands westward. But Southern Democrats were against it because it meant more new States opposed to slavery—and thus more " Black Republicans " in the Senate. So this, too, failed—after a vote on sectional lines.

And the same was true of the tariff. Unemployment was widespread in Pennsylvania because the British ironworkers could undersell the American, and it was spreading in New England because the British textile workers could do the same. Yet the South, with its cotton and tobacco selling at world prices, wanted cheap goods from abroad rather than expensive goods from New England.

The tariff problem is a nuisance to politics at any time. But it becomes a veritable curse when a very large nation divides on geographic as well as class lines, when the factories are all in one region and the plantations in another. In February 1859, the Senate refused to increase the duties. Promptly the manufacturers of Pennsylvania announced that they would organise their region for the Republicans, in return for binding promises of protection. This meant that Lincoln's western friends, who were still indifferent to the tariff, must accept it for the sake of votes. It meant that the Republicans would probably win the presidency in 1860. Did it also mean

*Plate 6.  Lincoln's home in Springfield, Illinois, a few days after the funeral*

*Plate 7. The Lincoln statue in Parliament Square, London*

that the nation—already split on every major issue—
would break into two pieces?

In February 1860, at the Cooper Institute in New York
City, Lincoln said all that could be said in honesty and
statesmanship to dissuade the South from secession.

## IX

This was Lincoln's most reassuring and careful speech,
and the one that did the most to gain him the nomination
for the presidency. The leading newspaper-editors of
New York City were in the audience, and Lincoln knew
he was being tested as a possible candidate. He also
knew that the Republican Party was being blamed (and
might lose the next election) because the mad John Brown
had invaded Virginia with a little " army " of twenty-two
men, in the hope of starting a slave insurrection.

Southerners had long proclaimed that abolitionists
wanted such an uprising and hoped for the atrocious
horrors of San Domingo. And they insisted that all
Republicans were abolitionists. The latter statement was
absurd but the former was at least partially correct.
Gerrit Smith of New York, and Thomas Wentworth of
Higginson and Theodore Parker of Massachusetts, three
eminent abolitionists, financed and advised John Brown.
They were all accessories before the fact.

John Brown's raid made even moderate opinion in the
North wonder whether the new party was dangerous,
whether it was secretly on the side of the fanatics. Ralph
Waldo Emerson might call Brown " a new saint awaiting
his martyrdom, and who, if he shall suffer, will make the

gallows glorious like the cross." But the politicians knew that even a taint of abolitionism brought defeat in a national election.

So Lincoln had two tasks in his speech at the Cooper Institute: to impress himself upon the East, and to save his party from the disrepute of the anti-slavery extremists. His tone was so conservative that his friends in the West were disappointed, and he himself said he did not blame them. But a member of the Young Men's Republican Union, under whose auspices he spoke, wrote to Lincoln: " You and your western friends, I think, underrate this speech. It has produced a greater effect here than any other single speech. It is the real platform in the eastern states, and must carry the conservative element in New York, New Jersey, and Pennsylvania."

Again Lincoln said nothing about any Republican policy except opposition to slavery in the territories. Pennsylvania might promise her votes in return for a tariff, Iowa and Minnesota in return for free home-steads. That was all very well. When the campaign started the necessary promises would be made. But meanwhile the party must be held together, pending its first national victory. And only the slave-issue could do that.

Lincoln began with a review of history—which he alone could have made so simple and yet so detailed—in which he showed that the fathers of the American Constitution believed that Congress *did* have the power to prohibit slavery in the public domain. So much for Dred Scott.

" As those fathers marked it," (i.e. slavery) said

Lincoln, " let it again be marked, as an evil not to be extended, but to be tolerated and protected only because of and so far as its actual presence among us makes that toleration and protection a necessity. Let all the guarantees those fathers gave it, be, not grudgingly, but fully and fairly, maintained. For this Republicans contend, and with this, so far as I know or believe, they will be content." So much for John Brown.

He then begged the Southern people—" a reasonable and just people "—to use their imagination about Republicans, to stop denouncing them " as reptiles, or, at the best, as no better than outlaws." " You will grant a hearing to pirates or murderers," he said, " but nothing like it to ' Black Republicans.' "

He stated and reiterated that his party did not wish to interfere with slavery in the Southern States, or with the laws of those States in any fashion. " But you will not abide the election of a Republican President! In that supposed event, you say, you will destroy the Union; and then, you say, the great crime of having it destroyed will be upon us! That is cool. A highwayman holds a pistol to my ear, and mutters through his teeth, ' Stand and deliver, or I shall kill you, and then you will be a murderer!' "

In conclusion he pleaded with his own friends and followers to help him find a remedy for the hysteria which was undoing the Union: " Even though much provoked, let us do nothing through passion and ill-temper. . . . We must not only let them (the South) alone, but we must somehow convince them that we do let them alone. . . . Wrong as we think slavery is, we can yet afford to let it alone where it is, because that much is due to the necessity arising from its actual presence in the nation."

But sympathy, friendship, even pity for the South must not mean weakness in the face of plans for the spreading of slavery. " If our sense of duty forbids this, then let us stand by our duty, fearlessly and effectively. Let us be diverted by none of those sophistical contrivances wherewith we are so industriously plied and belabored —contrivances such as groping for some middle ground between the right and the wrong, vain as the search for a man who should be neither a living man nor a dead man."

What more could anyone say, or be prepared to do? Lincoln would accept existing wrongs which had been built into the structure of the Union, because he had learned in his lonely meditations that the choices of this world never lie between pure good and evil. He would stand implacably against the spreading of those wrongs into the newly-settled lands. " We must give them a clean bed," he said of the pioneers, " with no snakes in it." And he would trust that slavery, even in the Southern States, must die out gradually, through its inherent wickedness and inefficiency, if only the Union could be preserved.

Lincoln never wanted quick emancipation. He agreed with young Charles Francis Adams, Jr., of Massachusetts (the grandson of one President and the great-grandson of another), who wrote home while he was serving in the Union army during the Civil War: " Emancipation as a government measure would be a terrible calamity to the blacks as a race. . . . Emancipation as the result of an economic revolution destroying their value as agricultural machines would be a calamity, though less severe. ... The only transition to freedom absolutely beneficial to them as a race would be one proportioned in length to the length of their captivity, such a one in fact as destroyed villeinage in the wreck of the feudal system. ... The blacks must be cared for or they will perish, and who is to care for them when they cease to be of value? "

Lincoln was one of the few men who had faced this problem fearlessly, who had thought painfully, steadily, about the future of the Negro. Therefore he was hated by the abolitionists, reviled by the slave-owners.

The reporter from the New York *Tribune*, after the meeting at the Cooper Institute, said that Lincoln was the greatest man since St. Paul. The *Tribune* announced that " no man ever before made such an impression on his first appeal to a New York audience." Yet Lincoln made no impression upon the Southerners whom he implored not to think evilly of all Republicans, and very little upon the Republican leaders whom he implored not to think evilly of the South. Humility, forbearance, moral elevation, were not the order of the day.

## X

Why, then, was Lincoln nominated for the presidency in May 1860?

When the Republican National Convention met at Chicago (which had become a city of 110,000 people) the Democrats had already met, and had ruined their election-chances by refusing to agree on Stephen A. Douglas as a candidate. The "fire-eaters" hated Douglas because he had insisted that the Dred Scott decision need not make slavery safe in a territory—some of them being glad of an excuse to split the Democratic Party as a step towards splitting the Union. When the Democrats adjourned their Convention until June, with nothing done, the happy Republicans foresaw that their foes must divide into two hostile camps.

So the delegates at Chicago felt victory in the air. Their first step was to contrive one of the most coherent platforms in American history: defence of the Union; prohibition of slavery in the territories; condemnation of the Dred Scott decision; a Pacific railway and other internal improvements; a homestead act; and a higher tariff.[1]

Platforms are seldom simple or sensible. Parties usually have to omit any plan which might lose votes in any large area. So they end by omitting almost everything, except unkind comments on the other party. But the Republicans were lucky in 1860. They were a sectional party by necessity. They had only to satisfy the North-west, the middle States,[2] and New England—regions whose interests did not seriously clash. Even so, they said nothing about the National Bank: the one item in the old Whig programme which might have been unpopular with some potential Republicans.

The same rule which makes most American platforms vague and turgid makes most presidential candidates

---

[1] The "platform" is the party programme, the list of promises for the coming campaign.

[2] Ohio, Pennsylvania, New Jersey, and New York.

relatively obscure. A man who has been at the centre of many political fights is likely to have made enemies in some States which the party cannot afford to lose. His views and his associates will be too well known for his own good.

When the Chicago Convention turned from the platform to personalities, to the choice of the one man to symbolise the entire movement, they found that even as a regional party they were large enough to have the old rule apply. In fact, it applied rigorously to the two most renowned candidates: Senator Seward of New York and ex-Senator Chase of Ohio.

This is what Lincoln had in mind when he wrote to an Ohio delegate just before the Convention: " My name is new in the field, and I suppose I am not the first choice of a very great many. . . . Our policy, then, is to give no offense to others—leave them in a mood to come to us if they shall be compelled to give up their first love." [1]

Lincoln was sufficiently known, but not known too well. Except for his opposition to the Mexican War, and for his stand on slavery (which was of course an asset), he had been in no passion-rousing fights. He was cautious, unlikely to make mistakes during a campaign, conservative enough for Pennsylvania, New Jersey, and New York, anti-slavery enough for New England and the West. Best of all (as he had shown in his campaign against Douglas) he could win votes in the Southern counties of Illinois and Indiana (where the settlers were

[1] Lincoln had told his supporters at the Convention, " make no contracts that will bind me." This they cheerfully ignored—with results which we shall see later.

mostly from Virginia and Kentucky), thus making victory possible in those vital States. So on the third ballot, when the delegates had paid their respects to "their first loves," Lincoln was nominated.

A few of the men who voted for him may even have guessed that he was wise, magnanimous, patient, and possessed of a genius for getting good work out of proud, self-confident subordinates.

## XI

The following month the Democratic Party split in two. The Northern delegates nominated Douglas, who stood by his own doctrine of popular sovereignty in the territories. The Southern delegates nominated John Breckinridge of Kentucky, with a platform demanding federal protection for slavery in every territory.

Meanwhile another party had been born: the Constitutional Union Party. This consisted of some ageing Northern Whigs (the last of the friends of Webster and Clay) who found the Republicans too radical for their taste, and some Southern Whigs in the border States who could not join a Northern, sectional party and who would not join the "fire-eaters" in destroying the Union.

When the campaign began, therefore, the nation had three sectional parties: the Republicans, and both halves of the Democrats. A few very tired and outmoded Whigs were the only group with a footing on each side of what was rapidly becoming a frontier.

As it happened, the break within the Democratic

Party did not matter. Lincoln would have been elected if all the anti-Republican votes had gone to one man—for he won every Northern State, including California and Oregon. Breckinridge won every State which was to join the Confederacy, except Virginia and Tennessee.[1] Douglas and the Constitutional Union candidate divided the remaining border States between them.[2]

The next question was whether Lincoln could induce the South to accept a Republican President—even provisionally, until he could be judged by his deeds. Although Lincoln seems to have thought this possible, there was never a real hope. All through the campaign the South insisted that a Republican victory meant secession. Lincoln would bring emancipation, said the Charleston *Mercury*: " It is loss of liberty, property, home, country— everything that makes life worth having." And the Richmond *Enquirer* proclaimed: " Resistance to wrong and injury—to tyranny, whether of one man or eighteen

[1] He also won Delaware and Maryland, slave-holding States which did not secede.

[2] The American does not vote for his presidential candidate directly. He votes, in the State of his residence, for his party's list of " electors." Each State has as many electors as it has members of Congress. (In 1860 for example, New York had 35 whereas Florida had three.) In any State, if a party wins by even one vote, all the electors go to the party's candidate. So if the Republicans won New York by a single vote in 1860, the 35 electors would all go to Lincoln. Whereas if the Breckinridge Democrats won Florida by 150,000, Breckinridge would still get only three electoral votes.

This is approximately what happened. Lincoln (or his electors) had narrow majorities in the populous States with large electoral votes, and received no votes at all in ten Southern States with small electoral votes. In all he received 1,800,000 votes, and his opponents together received 2,800,000. But Lincoln received 180 *electoral* votes, whereas all his opponents received only 123.

millions—is the cherished birthright of every citizen of the Federal Union."

The years of hysteria had done their work. Even the Southern unionists—a large minority, and in some States perhaps a majority—warned the North that the " fire-eaters" had stirred passions which nobody could control. And so it proved.

Immediately after the election the legislature of South Carolina called a convention which met in December 1860, and voted unanimously for secession. Within six weeks South Carolina had been joined by Mississippi, Florida, Alabama, Georgia, Louisiana, and Texas. And in February 1861 (a month before Lincoln took office), they formed themselves into the Confederate States of America, with Jefferson Davis as provisional President and Alexander Stephens as Vice-President.[1]

No good can come from re-arguing the question: Did the South have a " right " to secede? President Lincoln and President Davis were both convinced that they were acting under the true Constitution of the United States and that they were justified by the most obvious facts of history. But in the end, the test of sovereignty is power. Clearly the South had a " right " to secede from the Union of President Buchanan, since the weary dispirited old man did not interfere. What remained to be seen was whether Abraham Lincoln—to whom the Union was a sacred trust—could persuade the North that secession was intolerable and that the nation must be reborn in blood.

[1] Virginia, North Carolina, Arkansas and Tennessee seceded later, after the fighting had begun.

# * 3 *

## The Years of Fulfilment
### *1861-1865*

FROM NOVEMBER until March, from his election until his inauguration, Lincoln had to watch impotently while the Buchanan administration disintegrated, while the Confederate States came into being, while federal property throughout the South was seized with no resistance offered. Lincoln (a mere President-elect) could not even give a direction to public opinion—and Buchanan would not.

Large segments of Northern opinion were opposed to holding the Union together by force. One group wished to let the South go in peace, and another wished to tempt her back into the Union by offering the hope of new slave-territories and States. When consulted as to his future policy Lincoln could make no pronouncements, because his policy must depend upon what he could persuade the public to support. No President could peremptorily order the men of the North to make war upon their fellow Americans.

But when asked for his own views and principles, Lincoln was brief and positive. He quoted President Jackson: " Our Federal Union, it must be preserved."

And he wrote to a supporter: " Prevent, as far as possible, any of our friends from demoralizing themselves and our cause by entertaining propositions for compromise of any sort on ' slavery extension ' . . . On that point hold firm as with a chain of steel."

Though conciliatory by nature, and sympathetic to the problems of the slave-holders in their own States, Lincoln would not budge from the stand he had taken at the Cooper Institute. If the South refused to trust him he could do no more. So far as it lay in his power, the Union would be preserved and slavery would not spread.

But would he come to office in time to have a say in the matter? Or would he find himself, on March 4th, the President of a people who had lost their will to act, lost their sense of destiny, because in a time of trouble they had nobody to rally them except Buchanan?

Ten days before his inauguration Lincoln met with delegates from twenty-one States who were attending a so-called Peace Conference and who still hoped to restore unity without fighting. The New York delegate said to Lincoln: " It is for you, sir, to say whether the whole nation shall be plunged into bankruptcy; whether the grass shall grow in the streets of our commercial cities."

" A sad but stern expression swept over Mr. Lincoln's face," wrote the delegate from Vermont. " ' I do not know that I understand your meaning, Mr. Dodge,' he said without raising his voice, ' nor do I know what my acts or my opinions may be in the future beyond this. If I shall ever come to the great office of President of the United States, I shall take an oath. I shall swear that I will . . . to the best of my ability, preserve, protect,

and defend the Constitution of the United States. . . .
It is not the Constitution as I would like to have it, but
as it *is*, that is to be defended. The Constitution will
not be preserved and defended unless it is enforced and
obeyed in every part of every one of the United States.
It must be so respected, obeyed, enforced, and defended,
let the grass grow where it may.' "

Mr. Dodge of New York was not alone in worrying
about bankruptcy, and the effects of war on "our
commercial cities." In January 1861, the mayor of New
York had cheerfully suggested to his council that when
the South had completed her Confederacy New York
City should leave the Union and become a free port!
"With our aggrieved brethren of the slave States," he
said, "we have friendly relations and a common sympathy. . . . Why should not New York City, instead of
supporting by her contributions two-thirds of the expenses
of the United States, become also equally independent?
As a free city, with but nominal duty on imports, her local
Government could be supported without taxation upon
her people."

Waiting for the days to pass, Lincoln must have
wondered what there would be left for him to take over,
when his time came. Yet his purpose was settled. If
he came to office—if he was not murdered first—he
would seek to have the Constitution obeyed "in every
part of every one of the United States." And this, as he
must have known, meant war.

We can imagine the pain with which Lincoln reached
such a decision. He could not persuade himself that the
war, when it came, would be easy. And he knew the

grim fact that war seldom makes anything better, often makes everything worse—but he also knew that this does not excuse man for bowing before evil. And to Lincoln, the destruction of the Union was a mighty evil. If permitted, it would frustrate " the last, best hope of man " by proving that even lucky America, unthreatened from without, could not hold a few scattered States together in the name of freedom—in the name of that Declaration of Independence which he said was the source of all his politics.

" We hold these truths to be self-evident, that all men are created equal, that they are endowed by their Creator with certain unalienable rights, that among these are life, liberty and the pursuit of happiness ": that is what the Union meant to Lincoln. He often put the same thoughts briefly in his own words: " As I would not be a *slave*, so I would not be a *master*. This expresses my idea of democracy."

Lincoln had lived too long with Carlyle's " great Fact of Existence " to believe that the Declaration of Independence had come true, or was ever likely to do so. But while the Union lasted, so did hope. The flag was flying, even if the men who sheltered under it were the customary mixture of good and bad. Lincoln would not know how to lower that flag.

Nevertheless, although he defended the " last, best hope " in the line of duty, he was not an easily hopeful man. He liked to quote the fable of the Eastern sages who had found one sentence which was always appropriate: " And this too shall pass away." He told an audience in Cincinnati (perhaps a shocked audience of

American optimists): " How much it expresses! How chastening in the hour of pride! How consoling in the depths of affliction! ' And this too shall pass away! ' "

Lincoln had no illusions about war. He did not think, as some Americans have seemed to think, that war is a game which one wins or loses, and that when it is over one goes home cheered or depressed, as the case may be, with the score settled for good.

He knew that all wars are a form of politics. He knew that all wars, if fought to a finish, are lost by both sides. He knew that the victorious survivors can never return to the same homes which they left and which they were defending, since the pious act of defence must already have bred new troubles and new dangers in the place of those which it defeated. He knew that war (like faith) may move mountains, but that war (unlike faith) does not dispose of the mountains: it merely pushes them from one place to another—from Germany to Russia, from Japan to China, from the problem of Southern secession to the problem of Northern revenge. He knew, nevertheless, that the appeal to force may be necessary. He knew almost too much for a President, who may have to pretend that he is God for a moment and choose between war and peace.

As we saw with President Polk, the American Congress alone has the Constitutional " right " to declare war; but the President (if he accepts his burdens for good reasons or bad) has the Constitutional *duty* to avoid or to create it. Sometimes a President may wisely (or unwisely) wait, hoping for the best, leaving the enemy to make the decision: the Kaiser's unrestricted submarine warfare in 1917; Pearl Harbour in 1941. But Abraham Lincoln was given no such choice. He had to take the plunge alone and uncomforted.

## II

Lincoln was even more lonely than most Presidents, for he did not truly feel at home in this world or the next. He could joke with friends or with strangers, but he could not speak his heart: " everybody knew him and nobody knew him." Secretive, unable to ask advice or sympathy, with a formal family life which gave no protection from the slings and arrows of fortune, he walked by himself, sunk in meditation, holding the world at bay with his droll stories.

Such a man is doomed to melancholy unless he is upheld by faith. And Lincoln seems never to have found such consolation. " I know there is a God," he said in 1860, " and that He hates injustice and slavery. I see the storm coming and I know that His hand is in it. If He has a place and work for me I believe I am ready." But this was a more confident statement than Lincoln could usually make. His friends testify that it worried him and made him restless to be asked to define his beliefs. " Probably it is my lot to go on in a twilight," he said, " feeling and reasoning my way through life, as questioning, doubting Thomas did."

In the heat of party politics Lincoln was frequently called an infidel. Yet he said: " If the church would ask simply for assent to the Saviour's statement of the substance of the law: ' Thou shalt love the Lord thy

God with all thy heart, and with all thy soul, and with all thy mind, and thy neighbour as thyself,'—that church would I gladly unite with." His wife summed up his divided soul as follows: " He never joined a church, but still he was a religious man. But it was a kind of poetry in his nature, and he never was a technical Christian."

The Bible, which he loved and made intimately his own, may have been chiefly a book of poetry for Lincoln. Such majestic poetry, plus his natural pity and humility, plus a lifetime of contemplating clear-eyed that " great Fact of Existence," alone with his own soul: all this may explain his greatness. But it could not bring peace of spirit amid the mounting hatreds of the fifties, or when presiding over the long fratricidal war. Ten years before that war he exclaimed one day to his law-partner: "The world is deaf to hope, deaf to its own death struggle, made known by a universal cry, What is to be done ? Is anything to be done? Who can do anything? . . . Do you ever think of these things? "

Lincoln had thought of little else throughout the intervening years, and in 1861 he was called upon to find the answers. Both the military and the political problems must have seemed insoluble during those months of waiting before he could take charge and try his hand. A glance at the map [1] shows the military problem and the near impossibility of winning such a war. But the political problem was worse.

If the war was to be a prolonged and mighty effort, would the North endure the strain? Were the stakes great enough and obvious enough? Could he make people

[1] See page 109.

understand what the Union meant to freedom in America and in the world? Could he mould a public opinion strong to resist the neutralism of north-eastern merchants; the defeatism of many Southern sympathisers (with Southern blood) in Ohio, Indiana and Illinois; the pacifism of those who preached " Let the erring sisters go in peace? "

And what of the Border States, slave-holding but not yet Confederate? How many could he keep from joining the South? The difficult war would become impossible without the aid or at least the neutrality of Kentucky, Maryland, and Delaware. This meant that he would have to keep his Republican abolitionists quiet—something that no one else had been able to do.

And what of England? Her short term interest was to recognise a free-trade Confederacy. The South had the cotton and the English had the manufactured goods: the two regions were complementary. Could England be restrained from recognising the South? If not the war was lost, for there could be no blockade against the British fleet, no Northern superiority in equipment against the British factories.

To-day, in the after-glow of success, the Northern task looks almost easy. We tend to an ignorant impatience that the war lasted so long, and we wonder how the South could have hoped to win. But to Lincoln, waiting on events and measuring his difficulties, the responsibility for saving the Union must have seemed almost unbearable. (It is doubtful whether any other American could have solved even one of the problems mentioned above. They were all problems calling for the subtlest and most delicate political touch.)

## III

Lincoln's troubles were made no easier by his remarkable but quarrelsome Cabinet. This was undoubtedly a " Ministry of all the talents "; but it was also a Ministry of all the self-assertive.

Before Lincoln could hope to restore unity to his country he had to build some semblance of unity in that " loose aggregation of free thinkers ": the Republican Party. Nothing positive held the party together except the hope of office and a distaste for slavery. And even here, some Republicans were for outright abolition, some agreed with the cautious middle-of-the-road Lincoln, and some were ready at the eleventh hour to concede new territories to the South. Furthermore, the leader of almost every group in this " loose aggregation " was strong, ambitious, stubborn, and convinced that he was a better man than Lincoln.

The new President's first decision was to put aside all personal feelings, ignore all animosities, and build a Cabinet which might at least symbolise unity among these ill-assorted groups. He began by offering posts to the three most prominent presidential candidates whom he had defeated at Chicago:[1]

First, William H. Seward of New York, Secretary of State. Seward, an ex-governor of his State, had entered

---

[1] Lincoln's Cabinet-making is an education in the tangles of American politics. Most Presidents, to be sure, do not have to cope with a new party, wherein there is no background of loyalty; yet all Presidents have a similar problem to Lincoln's, because all major parties in America are loose coalitions of groups which stand for regional or class or business interests—and the Cabinet should contain a member from each important group.

the Senate in 1849 as a Whig. Friendly, sociable, a good companion and an inveterate gossip and story-teller, he became his party's leader in the Senate after the death of Clay and Webster. Tormentingly ambitious, his eye from the beginning had been on the White House.

Seward's father was the owner of three slaves (New York did not abolish slavery until 1827), and they became the boy's childhood friends. Perhaps they taught him to hate the institution which demeaned them. In any case, by the time he went to the Senate he was not only an ardent, partisan Whig but had made a national reputation through his attacks on slavery.

When the Whigs faded into insignificance Seward became a Republican, confident that he would lead the new party as he had led the old. Vain as well as ambitious, he was outraged at Lincoln's nomination; but he comforted himself that he would dominate Lincoln and become virtual Prime Minister of the administration, thus retrieving the errors of the Chicago Convention. " I have advised Mr. Lincoln," he wrote to his wife, " that I will not decline. . . . I shall try to save freedom and my country."

Second, Salmon P. Chase of Ohio, Secretary of the Treasury. Chase was a New Englander who had been taken West by his uncle and had settled in Cincinnati to practise law and politics. He was austere, overbearing, deeply religious in a sanctimonious fashion, and a high-principled abolitionist. He was also proud, selfish, and utterly convinced that it was his duty to become President. In vain pursuit of this duty he had joined almost every party: Whigs, Free Soilers, Abolitionists, Democrats, the anti-immigrant party which called itself " American," and finally (in 1856) the catch-all Republicans. In Lincoln's Cabinet he represented the abolitionist wing of the Democrats—the men who had left their old allegiance because of Kansas-Nebraska. Captious and scholarly, he was outraged by Seward's easy worldliness and by Seward's absurd notion that he was more important than Chase. (Lincoln, it was assumed, had no such pretensions.)

Third, Edward Bates of Missouri, Attorney General. Bates was an attractive figure out of the youth of the Republic. He was born in Virginia while George Washington was President, and lived there until he was twenty-eight. His wife was a South Carolinian and one of his sons fought in the Confederate army. He thought the Negro was his natural inferior and looked upon abolitionists (like Chase) as madmen if not traitors. But Bates, who was devoutly religious, thought slavery unchristian. He stood as strongly as Lincoln against the extension of such wickedness. And as a Whig he shared Lincoln's almost mystic view of the sanctity of the Union.

Missouri, the State of his adoption, was strongly Democratic. So Bates could not hope for a political career. But as a successful lawyer and leading citizen, wise and honoured, he became the sage of the South-west. He called himself an " old-fogy Whig." He had joined the party in the late twenties (almost before it was born), and he remained a member long after it had died. He never considered joining the Republicans, whose programme he approved: too many of them were what he called *Jacobins*, a word which reminds us of the far-off quarrels between Jefferson and Hamilton.

Yet Bates was a serious candidate at Chicago because the politicians from the " border States " warned that he was the one man whom the South might accept as a semi-Republican President. For the same reason Lincoln wanted him in the Cabinet, in order to help keep Missouri loyal to the Union—for the " border States " were vital to Lincoln's plans. Courteously (and perhaps with some awareness of Lincoln's greatness) Bates accepted the post. He resigned in 1864, when he could no longer bear to associate with a band of *Jacobins*.

Lincoln's next task was to find a prominent Republican from New England, and if possible an ex-Democrat—since the ex-Whigs were amply represented by Seward and Bates, whereas Chase was an abolitionist rather than a true Democrat. Luckily for posterity Lincoln chose Gideon Welles of Connecticut, the editor of the Hartford *Times* and one of the most vindictive diarists in American letters—who found ample material for his talent in this incongruous Cabinet.

Welles (who became Secretary of the Navy) was a Puritan by temperament: an ultra-Puritan in his love for examining his own faults and his neighbours'. He was honest, fearless, and a good judge of character. Alone among his colleagues he seems to have taken Lincoln's measure: in his most unflattering diary he often calls the President " that illustrious man."

A Jacksonian Democrat,[1] Welles joined the Republicans in 1856. He was unknown to the public but as a jour-

[1] The policies of President Jackson (1829-37) were popular democracy (making the President into a tribune of the people), no national bank, no internal improvements at federal expense—and the preservation of the Union.

nalist he had wide influence among politicians. Seward
had long hated him, perhaps because Welles regarded
Seward with an " icy revulsion "—a feeling which, when
Welles grew to know the Cabinet intimately, he extended
to most of its members.

The next appointment was made wholly with an eye
to the " border States "—for Lincoln was confident, as
we have said, that the Union must be defeated unless
the Northern tier of slave-holding States remained
faithful.[2] One family of great renown had influence in
three of those States: the Blairs, who came from Kentucky and who had settled in Maryland and Missouri.

There were three important Blairs in Lincoln's day.
First the father, the "Old Man of Politics," who had been
the friend, the daily adviser, and the devoted follower
of President Jackson. He was now an elder statesman in
affluent retirement in Maryland—but still the political
wizard of the Jacksonian " Brains Trust," to whom pru-
dent politicians still went for advice. He had given the
family house in Washington to his son Montgomery
—" Blair House," on Pennsylvania Avenue, now half
museum and half annex to the White House (and lately
the home of President Truman while the White House
was being repaired).

The other son, Frank Blair, was a lawyer and politician
in Missouri, risking his life daily in that turbulent State
by hot-headed anti-slavery speeches. When Frank Blair

[2] Delaware, Maryland, Kentucky, Missouri—all of which Lincoln saved
from the Confederacy. He could not hope for Virginia—but in 1863 the
Northern and western counties of Virginia seceded to the Union. From
the Atlantic Ocean to the border of Kansas, the Confederacy was thereafter
bounded by slave-States attached to the North.

campaigned for Lincoln in 1860 he was warned that he was almost sure to be assassinated. So he posted a challenge to any man at any time with any weapon—but he asked that it should be a duel and not an ambush.

The three Blairs were a unit—like a clan from the mountains of Kentucky. Together they befriended you; together they hounded you. And together they sought the advancement of all Blairs. In self-defence most politicians combined to resist this formidable tribe. But Lincoln had need of them. The father's name was magic to every old Jacksonian who had been taught by that great President to revere the Union. The Blair clan was strong in two border States and had roots in a third. So one of them—it didn't much matter which—must join the Cabinet. Montgomery Blair, of Maryland and the District of Columbia, became Postmaster General.

We now turn from high but practical politics to politics of a different kind. We have seen that Lincoln sent word to the Chicago Convention that no promises were to be made in his name. Nevertheless, to make sure of the Pennsylvania vote, his manager offered a Cabinet post to Senator Simon Cameron: an irascible, unscrupulous, party boss.

The best that can be said for Cameron is that he never tricked anybody into thinking well of him. He forced his way to power through brutality, not cunning. He did not even pretend to have an opinion on any subject except money. Although he spoke for Pennsylvania in the Senate from 1845-51, and from 1857 onwards, he showed no interest in slavery, or the Mexican War, or the

Wilmot Proviso, or Dred Scott. But he became the chief champion of a high tariff. He also founded the most long-lived political machine in American history, which dominated Pennsylvania from the days of Lincoln to the days of Franklin Roosevelt.

The testimony against Cameron is interesting for its quality and its unanimity. President Jackson said he " was not to be trusted by anyone in any way." President Polk said " he is a managing, tricky man in whom no reliance is to be placed." President Buchanan called him " an unprincipled rascal " and a " disorganizer." And Lincoln's advisers, when they heard that the appointment was contemplated, rushed to testify that Cameron was " a man destitute of honor and honesty " and " the very incarnation of corruption."

" I don't think he would steal a red hot stove," said a fellow-politician from Pennsylvania when asked about Cameron's honesty. Unwisely, an apology was demanded. " Oh well," came the answer, " I apologize. I said Cameron would not steal a red-hot stove. I withdraw that statement."

Nevertheless, Simon Cameron became Secretary of War. And an obscure ex-Congressman from Indiana, Caleb Smith, became Secretary of the Interior in payment of another promise made by Lincoln's manager at Chicago.[1]

Smith proved to be only a minor nuisance—weak, and somewhat absurd, and fertile in bad advice. After

[1] Not only were these two promises against Lincoln's orders and against the public interest, but they were unnecessary. We now know that the delegates from Indiana and from Pennsylvania would have voted for Lincoln in any case.

eighteen months Lincoln got rid of him by making him a federal judge. But Cameron did not last so long or go so quietly. The character witnesses were all proved right: corruption in the War Department was immediate, enormous, and steady. An outraged Congress collected three thousand pages of evidence, which it published in 1862. So in January of that year Lincoln sent Cameron as Minister to Russia, replacing him with another ex-Democrat: Edwin Stanton of Ohio.

Stanton was an angry, self-satisfied man who thought he should run the war single-handed: a man with a rough intolerant manner and a large administrative incapacity, but honest, hard-working, intelligent, and in the end a true "organizer of victory." Yet Stanton only became a good Secretary of War because of the leadership of the infinitely patient, infinitely calm Lincoln. Needless to say Stanton looked down upon Lincoln and talked insultingly, disloyally, about him.

We shall not have space to recount the antics of this strange, incompatible Cabinet, this uncanny background to Lincoln's years of trial. But there they all were: able, forceful, hating each other, conspiring against each other, working themselves to the limit for the cause but seldom agreeing as to the nature of that cause. And always among them, watching with malice, noting with accuracy and with a cold puritanical glee, was Gideon Welles with his enormous beard—Welles, who was to immortalise their shortcomings.

No wonder Lincoln sometimes took refuge in his only

self-indulgence: telling to the most unsuitable visitors his most unsuitable stories.

Sandburg recounts with pleasure the effect of these stories on some of the serious people who " didn't want a Laughing President. There never had.been a Laughing President. At the head of the government should be a solemn man who was constantly grave and dignified in his deportment. . . . For President there should be a man as earnest as the Constitution and the amendments thereto. If he should be so comical that he could make a cat laugh, he wouldn't do." [1] Luckily, right up to the end, there were still times when Lincoln could make a cat laugh. But they became fewer and fewer.

## IV

In his Inaugural Address, in March 1861, Lincoln put the choice for war or peace upon the South: " In your hands, my dissatisfied fellow-countrymen, and not in mine, is the momentous issue of civil war. The government will not assail you. You can have no conflict without being yourselves the aggressors. You have no oath registered in heaven to destroy the government, while I shall have the most solemn one to ' preserve, protect, and defend ' it."

This was not exactly true. In a war where both sides feel desperate, each side can always find grounds for believing that the other is the " aggressor." On this occasion the South fired the first shot; but the North

[1] *The Prairie Years*, vol ii, pp. 306-7.

took the steps which precipitated that act of " resistance." Indeed the North could do no other, under Lincoln's leadership.

We have seen that while Buchanan vaguely wavered between weakness and collapse, government property in the South was seized by the Confederate States: two forts in South Carolina, one in Georgia, one in Alabama—and in Florida both a fort and a navy yard. Fort Sumter in Charleston Harbour was the most important federal post which had not yet been abandoned. Buchanan had even sent a rescue ship to Sumter; but it was driven off by Confederate batteries. So there the matter rested, confused and dangerous, on the day Lincoln came to office. And the North waited to see whether the new President could summon more energy than the old. If not, the fort would be starved into submission within a few weeks.

Lincoln asked the members of his Cabinet for their opinions: should he provision Sumter, or let it fall? Seward and four others were for doing nothing. Blair was for action. And Chase hedged. So Lincoln was to all purposes alone (supported only by the youngest of his advisers) when he decided to send food to the garrison, risking the accusation that he thereby asked for war.

The Governor of South Carolina was officially informed of the expedition. Lincoln promised to land no reinforcements unless the ships or the fort were attacked. Yet on April 12th the batteries in Charleston Harbour opened fire on Fort Sumter. On the 14th the garrison surrendered, and on the 15th, Lincoln summoned 75,000 militia to put down the rebellion. Virginia, Tennessee,

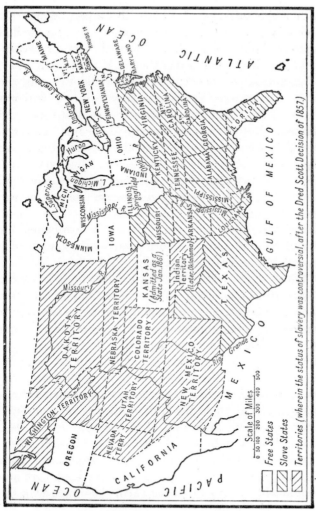

*The United States in 1861, when Lincoln became President*

North Carolina, and Arkansas thereupon joined the Confederacy and the bitter struggle began: nine million people in the States which had seceded,[1] against twenty-two million in the remains of the old Union.

The attack on the flag seemed briefly to unify the North. Later, when men found how long and hard was the task, a large minority wondered whether it was worth pursuing. But at first all was glory and fire. Lincoln, by taking positive action, had clearly done what his people wanted.

" The assault upon Sumter started us all to our feet, as one man," wrote Horace Binney on May 27th to a friend in England; " all political division ceased among us from that very moment." Then he explained (as Henry Clay and Lincoln had repeatedly explained) why peaceful secession was impossible:

" Some of the writers for the English press have but an imperfect knowledge of the necessities of the free States. . . . We are large enough, they say—and that is true enough, though nothing to the purpose. The North and West cannot conquer them (i.e. the Confederacy). That also may be true, and yet nothing to the purpose. *They* will conquer the North and West and destroy the Union, if they can bring about what these writers recommend. . . . They hold the Gulf of Mexico and the River Mississippi under their control, if they are left as they claim to be . . . Our intercourse with the Pacific States, all faithful to the Union, lies over the Isthmus of Darien (i.e. Panama). How can any part of the West continue in union with the North, or the Pacific be united with the

[1] Including 3,500,000 slaves.

Atlantic States, if an independent power holds this control? "

Northerners were not the only Americans who saw the facts of geography. Many Southerners dreamed of dominating the coasts and islands of that half-inland sea (into which flow all the majestic rivers of the Middle West), and there building a slave-society to rival Hellas. Robert Barnwell Rhett—the first of the fire-eaters, " the father of secession "—pictured the historian of the twenty-first century describing the brave deed: " And extending their empire across this continent to the Pacific, and down through Mexico to the other side of the great Gulf, and over the isles of the sea, they established an empire and wrought out a civilization which has never been surpassed or equalled—a civilization teeming with orators, poets, philosophers, statesmen and historians. . . ."

Here is indeed the dream of a classical revival:

> " *the purple dream*
> *Of the America we have not been:*
> *The tropic empire seeking the warm sea,*
> *The last foray of aristocracy.* . . ."

The Mexicans and the Caribbean islanders should have been thankful that the " tropic empire " was opposed by Abraham Lincoln, whose mother died of poverty and cold in Indiana. For Lincoln and the fire-eaters were agreed on one truth: if slavery were to be confined within the boundaries of 1861 it had no future. Aridity halted it to the West, politics to the North. Yet the old cotton lands were perishing under the one-crop system, while the black labour-gangs multiplied incontinently. If Lincoln had accepted secession, Mexico would soon have had a second taste of the gringo's " manifest destiny."

But Horace Binney explains why the Middle West could not (even in selfishness) permit this solution: she must not be denied the mouth of her river-system, or her access to the Pacific. Like most of his contemporaries, Binney assumed that a thousand miles of desert separated Kansas from California. Until the invention of barbed wire (about 1877) and the introduction of the tin windmill (about 1872), few men believed the " Great American Desert " to be habitable. If to-day we smile at the thought that we need the Isthmus of Darien to reach Los Angeles, we all admit that the Mississippi and its tributaries are still the veins of the body of the United States.

America has no double river-system like the Rhine and the Danube, emptying in opposite directions. The east and the west coasts are paralleled by mountains from which streams fall briskly into the sea. But between them is the Great Valley, more than two thousand miles wide, where the rivers (unless flooded) run sluggishly across the flat land, making for the Gulf of Mexico, and for the most part flowing first into the Mississippi. That river has forty-two tributaries, the longest being the Missouri (3,047 miles), the entire system containing 12,498 navigable miles. Here is the land-mass of the United States, seemingly designed by nature to be a unit. Here is what the Middle-Westerners in Lincoln's armies did not wish to see divided.

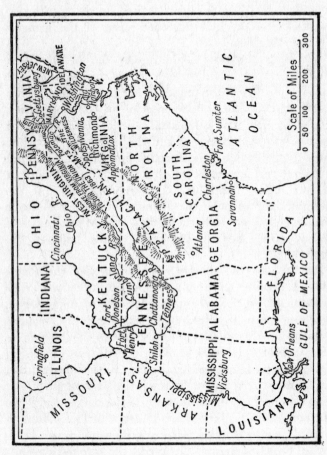

The Geography of the Civil War

## V

If the map of the United States is helpful in understanding why the war began, it is essential in understanding how the war was fought. The map shows that there had to be two wars—and that only a great Northern general with great resources behind him could hope to co-ordinate them. East of the Appalachian range (which rises in North Carolina to 7,000 feet and which is a formidable barrier all the way from Pennsylvania in the North to Central Georgia), Washington and Richmond, the rival capitals, faced each other across a hundred miles of rough country—some of it piedmont, some of it the forlorn Virginia " Wilderness ": flat, with scrub forest, almost uninhabited.

If the North took Richmond nothing would happen except that foreign recognition of the South would become less likely. The South was a loose Confederacy. Until the eve of Lee's surrender there was no unity of command. The Government at Richmond did not even have authority to control the railways for military purposes until February 1865—two months before the final collapse. Each Southern State fought its own war in its own way and had to be wheedled by the so-called Central Government to lend its armies temporarily to a central plan. Yet each State was absolute in its determination and could neither be frightened nor discouraged. There was scarcely room east of the mountains to obtain a decision against such a Confederation. Lee's army could be destroyed in this narrow corner—but not the South.

East of the mountains, however, the South might win —by taking Washington. This would impress the European mind, for Washington was a real capital which collected real taxes and had real authority over its armies. (In wartime, power is centralised in Washington as in a European capital.) The fall of Washington would probably have brought French and British recognition of the Confederacy, the end of the blockade, the end of Northern hopes. It would also have strengthened immeasurably the millions of defeatists, pacifists, and pro-Southerners with whom the North soon abounded. The South was strong in purpose, since it fought for its life. The North was weakened by faction, since it fought for an idea.

From 1861 to 1863 Lee's Army of Northern Virginia battled and manœuvred in this land between the mountains and the sea—battled to hold the Union forces at bay, manœuvred for a chance to strike north into Maryland and outflank the Federal City. McClellan and Pope and the other generals who depressed and disappointed Lincoln during those years have been too much blamed for their caution in preserving their armies intact. They could lose the war in a day; but they had small hope of winning it by mere victories in Northern Virginia.

At last, in 1863, Lee's chance came. He took the offensive and marched to Gettysburg, Pennsylvania. He sought to do what was thus far impossible for the North —to end the war by one great strategical victory on the highest level. If he had conquered at Gettysburg,

Washington must have fallen and the South would probably have been acknowledged by Europe as an independent nation.

Lincoln had sent his best man to London—Charles Francis Adams, son of an American President and grandson of another—to avert such recognition. With the help of the cotton-textile workers of England, who saw the American war as a fight for freedom, Adams had been barely, precariously successful. A Southern victory at Gettysburg might well have defeated him. But unhappily for the Confederacy, Gettysburg was Lee's worst battle. The chance to win with one grand stroke eluded him. The Army of Northern Virginia received losses from which it did not recover.

West of the Appalachian range, meanwhile, the Union was winning the war on Lincoln's slow plan, the only safe plan available, the plan of cutting the huge Confederacy into bits and destroying it piecemeal. (The unfolding of this plan drove Lee to his superb gamble at Gettysburg.) And in the West Ulysses Grant was in charge—the most enigmatic figure in American history.

The son of an Ohio tanner, Grant was trained at the United States Military Academy and became a professional officer. He fought in the Mexican War. (" I have never altogether forgiven myself," he said; " I do not think there was ever a more wicked war than that waged by the United States against Mexico.") In 1854, bored and lonely in a California post, he drank himself out of the army. During the next seven years he failed at farming, failed at selling real estate, failed as a clerk in a small-town leather store in Illinois. Yet when the war came he woke from his slack despondency and became a man of unbending purpose, with a grasp of detail which astonishes military historians. Why this transformation occurred, nobody knows.

Grant did not like war, and he hated armies. " I never went into the army without regret," he later said to Bismarck, " and never retired without pleasure." His wife was a slave-owner and he did not condemn slavery. " I have no hobby of my own in regard to the Negro," he wrote to his father in 1862, " either to effect his freedom or to continue his bondage." We must assume that the attack on the Union roused Grant's vast and long-somnolent powers.

The regular army did not want Grant back; but a friend in Congress got him an Illinois State commission and then induced Lincoln to make him a brigadier-general. At once he became a great military leader, although his ruthlessness with lives was such that public opinion might have destroyed him had not Lincoln stood firm.

In 1862 Grant captured Fort Henry on the Tennessee river [1] and Fort Donelson on the Cumberland. At the other end of the long river-system the Union navy took New Orleans. Then Grant (after suffering huge casualties in the drawn battle at Shiloh—his worst battle) moved south towards Vicksburg, the last Confederate strongpoint on the Mississippi. If Vicksburg fell the South would be cut in two and the Union would hold the river system of the Great Valley.

[1] See map, page 113.

There was a question, however, whether Grant would be allowed to besiege Vicksburg. The Union losses in the indecisive battle of Shiloh had been so shocking that the Northern press and politicians begged Lincoln to get rid of Grant.

One man of great political influence called at the White House to press for this dismissal. He found Lincoln exhausted, but patient as usual. The following account of the interview shows the unfair strain upon a man who has to be head of a government, guardian of a nation's conscience, and commander-in-chief at the same time:

" I appealed to Lincoln for his own sake to remove Grant at once, and, in giving my reasons for it, I simply voiced the admittedly overwhelming protest from the loyal people of the land against Grant's continuance in command. I could form no judgment during the conversation as to what effect my arguments had upon him beyond the fact that he was greatly distressed at this new complication. When I had said everything that could be said from my standpoint, we lapsed into silence. Lincoln remained silent for what seemed a very long time. He then gathered himself up in his chair and said in a tone of earnestness that I shall never forget: ' *I can't spare this man; he fights!* ' "

Lincoln had had his fill of generals who talked, of generals who played politics, of generals who made themselves the darlings of the press and explained persuasively why they did not fight. But Grant—" such a quiet little fellow," Lincoln called him—was a new experience. Perhaps he had too little regard for life; yet after the slaughter at Shiloh his stunned army moved forward towards Vicksburg. So even " an overwhelming protest from the loyal people of the land " could not bring Lincoln to unseat him. Nevertheless, it must have been a disconcerting war to conduct from the White House, when the public felt it had a right to sack the high command, when the Secretary of State and the Secretary of the Treasury were as enraged against each other as against the enemy, when half the Northern Democrats felt the war should never have been started and half the Republicans felt it was being fought for the wrong cause.

## VI

Grant's national fame was won at Vicksburg. For twelve discouraging months he attacked, with the help of Union gunboats; but every assault and every manœuvre was outwitted. Then daringly he crossed the Mississippi and moved his army south of Vicksburg. The gunboats and transports ran the Confederate batteries and re-ferried Grant's troops to the east bank, where the Union army was not only outnumbered but had no line of communications.

The gamble succeeded. Vicksburg surrendered on the 4th of July, 1863. On the same day the Confederate ambulance trains headed south from Gettysburg, and Lee's beaten army prepared to follow them home across the Potomac. Militarily, Vicksburg was the more decisive of the two battles. But we have seen that if Lee had won at Gettysburg the South might have gained the foreign recognition which alone could break the blockade. The peace-party in the North might then have become strong enough to compel early negotiations, which would have meant accepting secession. So no wonder the friends of the Union celebrated on that famous Fourth of July.

" We have had the dark hour," wrote William Lusk: " The dawn has broken, and the collapsed Confederacy has no place where it can hide its head. . . . Slavery has fallen, and I believe Heaven as well as earth rejoices."

The rejoicing was premature. Twenty-one months of hard fighting were still to come. But the North had learned that General Lee could be beaten. And in the West, Grant had given Lincoln the pleasure of proclaiming that " the Father of Waters again goes unvexed to the sea."

Four months later part of the battlefield at Gettysburg was made a permanent cemetery for the soldiers who had fallen there. The principal speech was a long-winded oration which nobody remembers. Then Lincoln was asked to make " a few appropriate remarks," which he did:

" Fourscore and seven years ago our fathers brought forth on this continent a new nation, conceived in Liberty, and dedicated to the proposition that all men are created equal.

" Now we are engaged in a great civil war, testing whether that nation or any nation so conceived and so dedicated can long endure. We are met on a great battlefield of that war. We have come to dedicate a portion of that field as a final resting place for those who here gave their lives that that nation might live.

It is altogether fitting and proper that we should do this.

"But in a larger sense we cannot dedicate—we cannot consecrate—we cannot hallow—this ground. The brave men, living and dead, who struggled here, have consecrated it, far above our poor power to add or to detract. The world will little note nor long remember what we say here, but it can never forget what they did here. It is for us the living, rather, to be dedicated here to the unfinished work which they who fought here have thus far so nobly advanced. It is rather for us to be here dedicated to the great task remaining before us—that from these honoured dead we take increased devotion to that cause for which they gave the last full measure of devotion—that we here highly resolve that these dead shall not have died in vain—that this nation, under God, shall have a new birth of freedom—and that government of the people, by the people, for the people, shall not perish from the earth."

## VII

As a result of Vicksburg the President put Grant in charge of all the Northern armies from the Appalachians to the Mississippi. One of these armies was on the verge of starvation at Chattanooga, across the Tennessee River from Georgia. By the close of 1863 Grant had not only saved the threatened troops—he had cleared the way for Sherman's march to Atlanta and to the sea.

At last, in time to plan the campaigns of 1864, Lincoln

made Grant supreme commander of all the armies of the United States. At last the war in the West and the war in Northern Virginia were to be co-ordinated. The North, as we shall see, might still have weakened on the political front and thus have accepted secession: the losses had been so heartbreaking, and during the grim years so many men had forgotten the purpose of the war. But from the military point of view, if the Union went on fighting the Confederacy was now lost.

Blockaded, denied recognition by France and Great Britain, with a glaring inferiority in munitions and a railway system which half-cancelled the advantage of interior lines, the South had nothing left except valour, stubbornness, and the immense distances over which her armies could retreat. But the South's assets failed to impress Grant. He was ready to spend the necessary men and take the necessary time—provided that Lincoln could supply him with those commodities.

East of the mountains (in May 1864) one Union army attacked Lee's front and another his communications. West of the mountains, under General Sherman, the army of Tennessee set out for Atlanta. There was to be no more rest for the Confederates—no more chance to substitute gallantry for munitions, enthusiasm for loco-motives.

When Grant assailed Lee and started torward Richmond he was coldly determined to keep the pressure mounting, however slow his progress and no matter what the losses—for he knew that he could afford it and that the enemy could not. He was out-fought in the two-day battle of the Wilderness; he was punished cruelly at

Spotsylvania Court House; and at Cold Harbour he suffered such losses that the Northern public was aghast. But he moved forward relentlessly to the siege of Richmond. In six weeks he lost 55,000 men, which was about the number of soldiers under Lee's command. Yet when he sat down before Richmond, Grant had more men in his army than when he started the campaign. Nothing could defeat such use of superior power, so long as the Northern will did not falter.

Sherman, meanwhile, had disappeared into the vastness of Georgia with an army of 110,000 men.[1] His job was to hammer the army of 60,000 (under Joseph E. Johnston) which opposed him, to cut the Confederacy into pieces (so that its armies could not reinforce each other but must die one by one), and to waste its resources like all the Four Horsemen combined (so that its armies should become as ragged and as hungry as men may be).

Johnston was a master of Fabian tactics, and for two months of retreat and manœuvre he avoided destruction —but he was forced steadily back towards Atlanta. When the city seemed doomed Johnston was replaced by the impetuous Hood, who at once delighted Sherman by taking the offensive. Hood was badly beaten, and, on September 2nd, Atlanta fell. Sherman sent about 50,000 of his men back to Tennessee. With the rest he set out eastward into the rich heart of Georgia— abandoning all communications—on his famous march to the sea.

Sherman's orders from Grant, at the start of the

[1] See map, p. 113.

campaign, had been to " get into the interior of the enemy's country . . . inflicting all the damage you can against their war resources." This he now proceeded to do, with a thoroughness which has never been forgiven in the South. For his men it was a picnic:

> *How the darkeys shouted when they heard the joyful sound!*
> *How the turkeys gobbled which our commissary found!*
> *How the sweet potatoes even started from the ground,*
>     *While we were marching through Georgia.*

For the Southern white men it was less amusing. On a sixty-mile front Sherman utterly ruined the towns, villages, farms, plantations, roads, railways, and bridges —all the way to Savannah on the sea, which is about two hundred and fifty miles from Atlanta. Then he turned north, carrying his devastation into South Carolina and up the eastern coast, between the mountains and the Atlantic. General Sherman wrote to his wife that the Southern people " regard us just as the Romans did the Goths and the parallel is not unjust."

Against a foe as stubborn as the Confederacy, who is possessed of such generals as Jackson, Lee, and the two Johnstons, these agonising tactics were doubtless necessary. But they put the maximum of strain on President Lincoln, who had to sustain the public's will to fight in what had come to seem an endless stultifying war—and in spite of one general whose victories cost him the total of the enemy's forces, and another general who vanished for months with a large army.[1]

[1] Sherman, however, reappeared most opportunely (with his victory at Atlanta) in time to influence the all-important election in the autumn of 1864. (See page 131.)

## VIII

Lincoln's persistence in proclaiming that his one aim was to save the Union—rather than free the slaves or to punish the " rebels "—angered the " radicals " in his own party. These radicals were a pugnacious alliance of three groups: first, the honest abolitionists who were shocked that slavery was still permitted in four loyal States (Missouri, Kentucky, Maryland, Delaware—and West Virginia after she joined the Union in 1863), and that it had not even been abolished by proclamation in the disloyal States; second, the political careerists who wished to free the slaves in order to ruin the South economically, thus breaking her power politically and ensuring long years in office for the Republicans; third, the men for whom war was merely an excuse for vindictiveness and who wished to punish and humiliate all slave-owners for the fun of feeling superior.

To the importunities of this mixed but influential crew, Lincoln gave two answers. The first is found in his letter to Horace Greeley of the New York *Tribune* (Aug., 1862):

"My paramount object in this struggle is to save the Union, and is not either to save or to destroy slavery. If I could save the Union without freeing any slave, I would do it; and if I could save it by freeing all the slaves, I would do it; and if I could save it by freeing some and leaving others alone, I would also do that. What I do about slavery, and the coloured race, I do because I believe it helps to save the Union; and what I forbear, I forbear because I do not believe it would help to save the Union. I shall do less whenever I shall believe what I am doing hurts the cause, and I shall do more whenever I shall believe doing more will help the cause."

The second answer depended upon the first: since the " paramount object " was to save the Union, Lincoln refused to be pushed into a step which must destroy it. The situation in Kentucky alone was enough to prove his wisdom. " To lose Kentucky is nearly . . . to lose the whole game," he had said; " Kentucky gone, we cannot hold Missouri, nor, as I think, Maryland. These all against us, and the job on our hands is too large for us. We would as well consent to separation at once, including the surrender of this capital." [1]

Yet Kentucky would have seceded immediately if Lincoln had interfered (quite unconstitutionally) with her slave system. The governor was a Southern sympathiser, and the people were almost equally divided between unionists and secessionists. Lincoln held them precariously, in a sort of friendly neutrality, by insisting that the war was only for the Union. If he had lost them, the frontier would have become the broad Ohio River all the way from Pennsylvania to the south-western tip of Illinois—to say nothing of the effect on Missouri and Maryland.

The war had scarcely started, however, when a Union general who was commanding in Missouri decreed the

---

[1] Washington, or the District of Columbia, is bounded by Maryland on three sides, by Virginia on the fourth.

liberation of all slaves belonging to Southern sympathisers. Lincoln withdrew both the decree and the
general—only to have another general, a year later,
issue a similar order for South Carolina, Georgia, and
Florida! When Lincoln countermanded that order
also, the abolitionists tried to organise a revolt against
the whole of his war policy. They were helped by the
fact that the war in Virginia had been going badly,
and that the press was beginning to demand a scape-
goat.

Lincoln saw that he must concede something to the
abolitionists, lest he be forced by public opinion into
conceding everything, and thus into losing the war.
After the drawn battle of Antietam Creek (September
1862), which at least ended a Confederate invasion of
Maryland and could be made to sound like a victory,
Lincoln announced that " persons held as slaves " within
areas in rebellion against the United States would be
proclaimed free on January 1st, 1863.

This was purely a war measure. Lincoln had no constitutional right to touch slavery in any State; but he
assumed the right to free the slaves of a rebel against the
Union—purely as a punishment for rebellion. Anyone
who ceased to rebel before January 1st would escape
the punishment.

Nothing was done—nothing could be done by the
President—to interfere with slavery in the loyal States.
And since the South went on fighting, the Emancipation
Proclamation had no effect in the rebel States. But it
quieted the abolitionists for the time being. And it
strengthened the hands of the British workmen, who had

opposed all plans to recognise the South and thus to break the blockade.

As if to prove Lincoln's political wisdom, and the folly of the radicals, Northern Democrats set up a clamour against this innocuous Proclamation. They would fight for the Union, they said, but not to deprive other men of property. And the legislature of Lincoln's own Illinois resolved that the Proclamation was

> " a gigantic usurpation, at once converting the war, professedly commenced by the administration for the vindication of the authority of the Constitution, into a crusade for the sudden, unconditional and violent liberation of 3,000,000 Negro slaves; a result which would not only be a total subversion of the federal Union but a revolution in the social organization of the Southern States, the immediate and remote, the present and far-reaching consequences of which to both races cannot be contemplated without the most dismal foreboding of horror and dismay."

Thenceforth Lincoln was opposed by two powerful groups within the Union. The radicals assailed him from the Left for not doing enough; the Democrats assailed him from the Right for doing too much. Some of the radicals demanded that the North arm the slaves, expropriate the rebels, desolate the South into a state of " hopeless feebleness," erase the old State lines and re-colonise the Confederacy. Some of the Democrats demanded that the war be brought to an immediate end, as an immoral failure.

Amid the mounting abuse of these two groups the

lonely President (with erratic support from his Cabinet) still sought to save the Union and to ensure humane treatment for the South. He announced that except for high officers of the Confederacy anyone would be granted an amnesty who took the oath of allegiance to the United States—and that when ten per cent of the people of any State had taken the oath they might hold elections and establish a State government. The radicals in the legislature forced through a bill declaring that the Congress, not the President, must set the terms for pardon and reconstruction; but Lincoln vetoed it.

The radicals then sought to deny Lincoln his renomination for the presidency in 1864, and to replace him with either Salmon P. Chase (Secretary of the Treasury) or with the general who had issued the slave-freeing proclamation in Missouri. Lincoln had little trouble in defeating these manœuvres: for all his humility and gentleness he was a politician who could see round most corners. He subsequently moved Chase to the Supreme Court and arranged for the final retirement of the general.

The Democrats, meanwhile, had nominated General George McClellan for the presidency. Robert E. Lee thought McClellan the best of the Northern generals. But he was one of those generals—with whom Lincoln was over-burdened at the beginning of the war—who never thought the time was ripe for fighting in Virginia. " Are you not overcautious," Lincoln wrote plaintively in October 1863, " when you assume that you cannot do what the enemy is constantly doing? " A month later

Lincoln retired McClellan for good, leaving him free to give all his time to politics.

The Democratic Party in 1864 consisted partly of " Copperheads " (who were opposed to continuing the war), and partly of men who believed that Lincoln was destroying the Constitution by his methods of conducting the war, by his use of troops to influence elections in the border States, and by his Emancipation Proclamation. McClellan's platform proclaimed a policy of peace:

" Resolved, that this convention does explicitly declare . . . that after four years of failure to restore the Union by the experiment of war, during which, under the pretense of a military necessity of war-power higher than the Constitution, the Constitution itself has been disregarded in every part, . . . justice, humanity, liberty, and the public welfare demand that immediate efforts be made for the cessation of hostilities, with a view of an ultimate convention of the States, or other peaceable means, to the end that, at the earliest practicable moment, peace may be restored on the basis of the Federal Union of the States."

In addition to being illiterate this was ridiculous, as Jefferson Davis quickly showed in his message to Lincoln (August 1864): " I shall at any time be pleased to receive proposals for peace on the basis of our Independence. It will be useless to approach me with any other."

No wonder Lincoln felt that a Democratic victory, on such a platform, would mean the end of the Union—unless the North could win the war before inauguraton day (March 4th, 1865). Yet the platform made a

skilful appeal to the war-weary—suggesting that if the
North would stop fighting to restore the Union, the
Union would magically restore itself. In August, Horace
Greeley predicted that Lincoln's defeat was certain; and
Lincoln wrote: "This morning as for some days past, it
seems exceedingly probable that this administration will
not be re-elected."

At that time Grant was suffering fearsome casualties
in the Wilderness. Sherman was missing, "somewhere
in Georgia." Then suddenly Atlanta fell. And Grant,
in spite of his losses, kept moving forward. Although
Sherman was about to disappear again (between Atlanta
and the sea), the North now knew that he could be
trusted to strike deadly blows. On election day (November 8th, 1864) Lincoln won 2,216,067 votes, McClellan
1,808,725. The vote in the electoral college was overwhelmingly for Lincoln.

While the President was watching the returns on that
fateful night, a friend pointed with malicious pleasure to
the defeat of two "especially malignant" Congressmen.
"You have more of that feeling of personal resentment
than I," said Lincoln. . . . "A man has not time to
spend half his life in quarrels." If Lincoln had taken
time to worry about what Senators or Representatives
called him he would have had no energy for the war.


## IX

The Constitution of the United States ensures that the
Congress must be jealous of any strong President, because
the powers that are supposed to be balanced equally

between the two branches of government are in fact largely in the President's hands during an emergency, if he chooses to use them. Although the President cannot legislate, he can *act*—and if the nation is in danger the public will support his action and the Congress must trot along behind, accepting events ungraciously.[1]

Lincoln took full advantage of the elasticity of his powers. He received more than his full share of abuse in Congress and in the opposition press. And there was justification for the feeling that he was too high-handed. He admitted that he had strained the Constitution in order to save it: " I felt that measures, otherwise unconstitutional, might become lawful by becoming indispensable to the preservation of the Constitution through the preservation of the nation. Right or wrong, I assumed this ground and now avow it."

The powers which Lincoln assumed after the attack on Fort Sumter were derived from two articles in the Constitution—one of which made him commander-inchief of the armed forces, the other of which gave him the duty " to take care that the laws be faithfully executed." From these clauses he deduced an authority to do whatever was needed to put down " insurrection."

Congress was not in session when Fort Sumter fell— doubtless to Lincoln's relief, since he wished to act, not argue. On the assumption that the Confederacy had started an insurrection, and not a foreign war, Lincoln

---

[1] But if the nation is not in danger, or does not know it, the Congress is an effective check, and can thwart executive action very much as the authors of the Constitution intended. A President can only expand his powers when the people are roused to demand action.

summoned the militia by executive act, proclaimed a blockade, expanded the regular army beyond the legal limit, paid the new troops without a congressional appropriation, suspended the privilege of *habeas corpus* (in spite of vehement opposition from the Chief Justice of the Supreme Court), and ordered a number of arrests on the suspicion of disloyalty. He also began a war against the South.

He then called Congress into special session (unless he had done so it could not meet for five months) and asked for the ratification of his acts—which in due time was forthcoming.

In his message to the special session (July 1861), Lincoln made his finest plea for the preservation of the Union. " This issue embraces more than the fate of these United States," he said. " It presents to the whole family of man the question whether a constitutional republic or democracy—a government of the people by the same people—can or cannot maintain its territorial integrity against its own domestic foes. . . . It forces us to ask, is there in all republics this inherent and fatal weakness? Must a government of necessity be too strong for the liberties of its own people, or too weak to maintain its own existence? . . . It is now for them (the people of the Union) to demonstrate to the world that those who can fairly carry an election can also suppress a rebellion."

This is the problem with which the federal republic had been wrestling from the beginning. It might have been solved by consent; but in view of the pugnacity of human nature, and the magnitude of the economic interests involved, it was always more likely to be solved by revolution: by a violent act of secession which was either accepted as unbeatable or resisted on the field of battle.

Although Congress had ratified Lincoln's belligerent deeds, the Supreme Court might still have declared them unconstitutional! The test came when a group of ship-owners—whose vessels had been seized during the interval between Lincoln's proclamation of a blockade and Congress's recognition of the war—sued for the recovery of their property. They claimed that a blockade is an act of maritime war, for which Lincoln had no authority. There could be no war until Congress acted. Lincoln's blockade was therefore illegal.

The case was very nearly lost by the government. In 1863, with the nine Justices divided five to four, the Supreme Court decided to reject the " anomalous doctrine . . . that insurgents who have risen in rebellion against their sovereign, expelled her courts, established a revolutionary government, organized armies, and com-menced hostilities, are not enemies because they are traitors."

The narrow majority reminds us of the troubles of a chief executive who has to get something done under the American Constitution.

## X

The most startling sign of the authority which Lincoln was willing to assume, in silence and on his own respon-sibility, was his plan for getting the South back into the Union without the interference of Congress. He was murdered the day on which he disclosed this plan to the Cabinet. Had he lived, and had he succeeded, the South would have been saved twenty-five years of revengeful exploitation, the North twenty-five years of shame—and the Negro might have been saved a large part of the mistreatment which still pursues him.

General Lee had surrendered five days before this final Cabinet meeting, and though other Confederate forces were still in the field the war was virtually over.[1] Lincoln's thoughts had already turned to assuagement. He said it was "providential" that the rebellion was crushed just after Congress had adjourned. The executive would not be hindered and embarrassed in making peace. "If we were wise and discreet," he said (according to Secretary of the Navy Gideon Welles), "we should reanimate the States and get their governments in successful operation, with order prevailing and the Union re-established, before Congress came together in December."

In 1861 Lincoln had presented Congress with a three-months'-old war which it could scarcely reject. He now hoped to present it with a peace which it could not upset. No treaty was necessary, so he had no need to consult the Senate. He could revert to his insurrection-theory: "this great rebellion," he called the war in talking to his Cabinet. The executive could set the terms for ending a "rebellion." And Congress could not meet until December, unless the President were to call a special session. Lincoln had more than seven months in

---

[1] About 260,000 men had died in the Confederate armies, out of a white population of less than six million. About 360,000 men had died in the Union armies, out of a population of twenty-two million.

which to restore his beloved Union, to " re-animate " the ex-Confederate States—and we have seen the generous terms on which he proposed to get them quickly back into the fold.[1]

A month before he died, in his second inaugural address, Lincoln had reaffirmed his vision of a truly magnanimous war. He could at last afford to turn his mind from military worries and to reflect on the meaning and the moral of the tragedy. After a brief reminder of why it had been right to accept war rather than let the Union perish, Lincoln added:

" Neither party expected for the war the magnitude or the duration which it has already attained. Neither anticipated that the *cause* of the conflict might cease with or even before the conflict itself. Each looked for an easier triumph and a result less fundamental and astounding. Both read the same Bible and pray to the same God, and each invokes His aid against the other. It may seem strange that any men should dare to ask a just God's assistance in wringing their bread from the sweat of other men's faces, but let us not judge, that we be not judged. The prayers of both could not be answered. That of neither has been answered fully. The Almighty has His own purposes. ' Woe unto the world because of offences; for it must needs be that offences come, but woe to that man by whom the offence cometh.' If we shall suppose that American slavery is one of those offences which, in the providence of God, must needs come, but which, having continued

[1] See page 129

through His appointed time, He now wills to remove, and that He gives to both North and South this terrible war as the woe due to those by whom the offence came, shall we discern therein any departure from those divine attributes which the believers in a living God always ascribe to Him? Fondly do we hope, fervently do we pray, that this mighty scourge of war may speedily pass away. Yet, if God wills that it continue until all the wealth piled by the bondsman's two hundred and fifty years of unrequited toil shall be sunk, and until every drop of blood drawn with the lash shall be paid by another drawn with the sword, as was said three thousand years ago, so still it must be said, ' The judgments of the Lord are true and righteous altogether.'

" With malice toward none, with charity for all, with firmness in the right as God gives us to see the right, let us strive on to finish the work we are in, to bind up the nation's wounds, to care for him who shall have borne the battle and for his widow and his orphan, to do all which may achieve and cherish a just and lasting peace among ourselves and with all nations."

Lincoln might have done it. He might have made a chivalrous peace in spite of the decrease in national honour which the long war entailed; for he was " gentle, plain, just and resolute." He might have bound up the nation's wounds with such wisdom and such elevation of spirit that when Congress reassembled the evil-doers in that body would have found themselves thwarted: the

Plunderers, and the Prigs, and the pure Vindictives alike. The South would then never have learned how much more terrible than Sherman's army was the post-war rage of the demagogue and the *embusqué*.

Lincoln was killed on the evening of April 14th, 1865, by John Wilkes Booth, a half-demented actor from Maryland who thought he was avenging the South. In fact he was condemning her to a long subjection.

After the years of fighting and suffering and profiteering and mud-slinging, after the roughness and demoralisation of war, this was no time for America to lose the man whom Walt Whitman called " the sweetest, wisest soul of all my days and lands."

# Epilogue

THE FUNERAL train took Lincoln's body on a wide route of fifteen hundred miles—through Baltimore, Philadelphia, New York, Cleveland, Chicago—back to Springfield, back to the stark prairie which had bred him. Everywhere the people mourned unrestrainedly:

> " *Through day and night with the great cloud darkening the
>      land,*
>   *With the pomp of the inloop'd flags with the cities draped
>      in black,*
>   *With the show of the States themselves as of crêpe-veil'd
>      women standing,*
>   *With processions long and winding and the flambeaus of
>      the night,*
>   *With the countless torches lit, with the silent sea of faces
>      and the unbared heads, . . .*
>      *O powerful western fallen star!* "

Thus he went home to be buried in the little prairie-town. That cruel land, " watered by the tears and enriched by the graves of her women," had given him steadiness and patience and a natural piety. Grierson in his memoirs describes a pioneer woman of Illinois:

" Moulded and subdued by the lonely days, the mono-
tonous weeks, the haunting hush of the silent nights, and
the same thoughts and images returning again and again,
she appeared as one who had conquered the world of
silence."

If a genius should arise in such a land it is fitting that
he should be thoughtful in the manner that all great
men from lonely places have been thoughtful, and that
he should make simplicity more beautiful than the brave
show of kings.

# Chronological Table

| Some events in Lincoln's Life | | Some events in British History | |
|---|---|---|---|
| 1809 | Abraham Lincoln born. | 1809 | Darwin, Tennyson, and Gladstone born. |
| 1816 | Lincoln family move to Indiana. | | |
| 1820 | Missouri Compromise. | | |
| | | 1825 | First railway opened in England. |
| 1830 | Lincoln family move to Illinois. | | |
| 1831–1837 | Lincoln at New Salem. | 1832 | First Reform Bill. |
| | | 1833 | Slavery abolished in British Colonies. |
| 1834 | Lincoln elected to Illinois legislature. | | |
| 1837 | Lincoln moves to Springfield, Illinois. | 1837 | Queen Victoria's Accession ; First steamboat from England to America. |
| 1842 | Lincoln marries Mary Todd. | | |
| 1846–1848 | Mexican War. | 1846–1847 | Irish Famine. |
| 1847–1849 | Lincoln in Congress. | 1848 | Revolutionary year in Europe. |
| 1850 | Clay's " Compromise of 1850." | | |
| | | 1853–1856 | Crimean War. |
| 1854 | Kansas-Nebraska Act. | | |
| 1857 | Dred Scott Decision. | 1857–1858 | Indian Mutiny. |
| 1860 | Lincoln elected President ; Secession begins. | | |
| 1861 | Lincoln's First Inaugural Address. | 1861 | Death of the Prince Consort. |
| 1863 | Battles of Gettysburg and Vicksburg. | | |
| 1864 | Lincoln re-elected President. | | |
| 1865 | Lincoln's Second Inaugural Address ; Lincoln Assassinated (April 14th, dies April 15th). | 1867 | Second Reform Bill. |

# A Note on Sources

1. The best one-volume biography is Benjamin P. Thomas's *Abraham Lincoln*. London, 1953.
2. The first important biography, which contains much source material, was by Lincoln's two secretaries: J. G. Nicolay and John Hay, *Abraham Lincoln*. 10 vols. New York, 1890.
3. Among the best of the recent books are:
    a. J. G. Randall, *Lincoln the President: Springfield to Gettysburg*. 2 vols. London, 1946. Vol. 3: *Midstream*. London. 1953.
    b. Carl Sandburg, *Abraham Lincoln: the Priarie Years*. 2 vols. New York, 1926. *Abraham Lincoln: the War Years*. 4 vols. New York, 1939 (The six volumes condensed into one volume: *Abraham Lincoln*. London, 1955).
    c. *Abraham Lincoln, his Speeches and Writings*, edited by Roy P. Basler. New York and Cleveland, 1946. (An excellent selection in 800 pages.)
4. Books which give the background for the years of Lincoln's emergence:
    a. Allan Nevins, *Ordeal of the Union*, 1847-1857. 2 vols. New York and London, 1947. *The Emergence of Lincoln*, 1857-1861. 2 vols. New York and London, 1950.
    b. Avery Craven, *The Coming of the Civil War*, New York, 1942.
5. For an understanding of the Civil War itself, the best book is *The Blue and the Gray: The Story of the Civil War as Told by Participants*. 2 vols. New York and Indianapolis, 1950. (Edited by Henry Commager.)

I would like to thank the following for permission to reproduce their photographs: the Illinois State Historical Library (plates 1, 2 and 6), the Radio Times Hulton Picture Library (plates 5 and 7) and Stefan Lorant for plates 3 and 4, which are taken from his *Lincoln, A Picture Story of His Life*.